EMDR for Anger Management

Somatic & Attachment-Focused Skills to Heal the Unresolved Trauma That Drives Your Chronic Anger

DEBORAH S. KENNARD, LLP

New Harbinger Publications, Inc.

Publisher's Note

This publication is designed to provide accurate and authoritative information in regard to the subject matter covered. It is sold with the understanding that the publisher is not engaged in rendering psychological, financial, legal, or other professional services. If expert assistance or counseling is needed, the services of a competent professional should be sought.

NEW HARBINGER PUBLICATIONS is a registered trademark of New Harbinger Publications, Inc.

New Harbinger Publications is an employee-owned company.

New Harbinger Publications, Inc.
5720 Shattuck Avenue
Oakland, CA 94609
www.newharbinger.com

Cover design by Amy Shoup

Acquired by Wendy Milstine and Jed Bickman

Edited by Rebecca Job

Library of Congress Cataloging-in-Publication Data on file

Printed in the United States of America

27 26 25

10 9 8 7 6 5 4 3 2 1 First Printing

"Deborah S. Kennard brings a creative and innovative focus to self-guided anger management with somatic and attachment-focused EMDR (SAFE). Her book is exceptionally well organized into two parts, with rich case examples, helpful exercises, and an overall theme of applied nonviolence. The thematic attention to SAFE also includes mindfulness awareness, compassionate assumption, healthy boundaries, and 'finding your answer.' I heartily recommend her book to anyone on a journey of self-discovery and healing."

—**Donald F. deGraffenried, LCSW**, EMDRIA-approved senior trainer in EMDR therapy with twenty-six years of experience

"In Deborah S. Kennard's *EMDR for Anger Management*, she offers a gentle but powerful approach that reframes the way we understand our own emotional struggles and anger issues. Her unique method opens the door to real change in a way that surpasses conventional therapies. This trauma-informed approach to anger management is so very needed, and this valuable resource is one I will be recommending to clients for years to come."

—**Gerry Crete, PhD, LPC**, founder of Transfiguration Counseling, and author of *Litanies of the Heart*

"Deborah S. Kennard's book is a refreshing and friendly primer on gaining agency and choice with difficult emotions and unpredictable circumstances. She does something very rare, welcoming readers with practical steps to shift easily from reactivity to genuine responsiveness and discovery. Lots of accessible examples and a can-do tone make this book essential for teens and those who care for teens."

—**Kathlyn Hendricks, PhD**, CEO and director of training at The Hendricks Institute, best-selling author, trainer, consultant, and host of the *be.play.love* podcast

"Powerful. Practical. Deeply compassionate. Deborah S. Kennard offers a breakthrough approach for moving past chronic anger so you can react in the present without being overwhelmed by the past. You'll come away with a profound understanding of how to draw on your strengths to see yourself and others with kind eyes so you can slow impulsive reactions, set appropriate boundaries, and find peace."

—**Eileen Kennedy-Moore, PhD**, author of *Kid Confidence*

"Who knew anger was the answer! Using real-life stories, metaphors, and plain language, the author guides the reader to understand how anger became the answer by applying EMDR therapy concepts. Unseen roots become seen as the reader follows the path forward. Relationships with oneself and others will settle (calm). This book is applicable to more than anger. I can see myself and other therapists recommending it to clients seeking therapy for a range of issues."

—**Regina Morrow Robinson, EdS**, therapist, EMDR trainer and consultant, and author of *EMDR Group Therapy*

"Praise for SAFE for anger management. Deborah S. Kennard's ability to relay complex topics about the impact of trauma on a person's ability to manage anger is refreshing. Filled with helpful exercises, case examples, and skill building, this book is an essential toolkit for anyone who wishes to transform their problematic anger and deepen their relationship to self and others. In a world of violence, Kennard offers a pathway to peace."

—**Ame Cutler, PhD**, founder of the Transgenerational Regeneration Institute, and author of *The Regeneration Process Method*

In memory of my amazing mother, Helen Robbins Paratore—her love, laughter, and dedication to her ten children changed a generational pattern of poverty and trauma. Her last piece of advice was "Enjoy life, that is the most important thing of all."

Contents

Introduction

SAFE EMDR and Anger

If you are reading this book, you likely already know that problematic anger can have devastating consequences. Maybe you've tried anger management techniques or even psychotherapy without relief. This book offers an alternative approach to managing the challenge of anger, which can be particularly helpful for those who have struggled the most with it.

Anger is a growing problem in our world and appears to be accelerating. It's often triggered by something external, leading you to believe that your anger is due to something outside of you. While it's true that an external event may act as a trigger, the source of the reaction lies within. The true root of anger is most often early, hurtful experiences—and often, the physical remnants of those memories are what activate your problematic anger. While there are many justifiable reasons for anger, the truth is, anger hurts—and it mostly hurts the person who is experiencing it.

Somatic and Attachment-Focused Eye Movement Desensitization and Reprocessing (SAFE EMDR) offers a step-by-step approach to extinguishing the root causes of problematic anger, providing an opportunity for personal transformation, freedom, and peace. In this book, you will be invited to take a different approach to your anger—and that approach includes appreciating the ways it has been helpful. Anger in itself is not a problem; we are all born with survival instincts, and anger is one of them. If you are threatened and you need to protect yourself or someone else, healthy anger gives you the energy for that protection. If your boundaries are violated, healthy anger offers a signal for you to take action. A healthy anger response appears when it's needed, then dissipates. However, if you are standing in a line at the bank seething with anger because it's taking so long, that is less about survival and more about patterned, habitual anger responses.

The residual effects of problematic anger span many areas of life. Chronic anger has real physiological and psychological effects, whether it is expressed or repressed. Chronic pain and illness, ulcers, depression, high blood pressure, adrenal fatigue, relationship issues, and other problems are all exacerbated (and may be caused) by the stress of living with the tension of unresolved, chronic anger.

This book may be helpful if you've experienced any of the following:

- Anger outbursts that result in feelings of shame or guilt
- Feelings of resentment and difficulty letting go of past experiences
- Hurting other people with your anger
- Worry about the effects of your anger on your children or others
- Chronic or unexplained physical tension, pain, or illness
- A desire to have a more peaceful life
- A readiness to take action and responsibility for your chronic anger
- A lack of success with other anger management methods

In 1996, I was introduced to Eye Movement Desensitization and Reprocessing (EMDR), a psychotherapeutic approach for processing traumatic experiences. I was trained in EMDR by its founder, Francine Shapiro, and gained firsthand experience of the EMDR process during training. I was so blown away by the effectiveness of EMDR on myself and my clients that I joined her faculty, eventually becoming an EMDR trainer myself. I developed Somatic and Attachment-Focused EMDR, or SAFE EMDR, as an expansion of Shapiro's Adaptive Information Processing Model (AIP). SAFE EMDR maintains the core principles of EMDR while making it more trauma-informed and user friendly.

After developing SAFE EMDR, I created the Personal Transformation Institute (PTI). Over the past nine years, I've trained thousands of clinicians across the world, many of whom have reported profound personal and professional growth through using these principles.

As I offer this book, I invite you to use it in whatever way works best for you. While EMDR therapy can only be done by a trained and licensed clinician, this book offers you an opportunity to understand and experience some of its principles, procedures, and methods. By reading and completing the exercises, you can better understand the origins of your anger and release some of the emotional burdens of the past. If you have a history of mental illness or significant trauma, I recommend working with an EMDR clinician alongside this book.

The Past Is Present

How your past affects you is less about what actually happened than it is about what you remember. Trauma continues to live in the present. If you have siblings, perhaps you've discussed your childhood memories and experiences, and discovered that you each remember them in a different way. There is a reason for this: it's the way human memory works.

Memory is not factual. Even if you and your sibling were both present for the same event, one of you may or may not have been completely present psychologically or physiologically. Or you may have been paying attention to different things, resulting in different memories of the same event. A pleasant memory for one sibling may feel overwhelming or traumatic to another. When feeling overwhelmed, we sometimes mentally distance ourselves from a situation; this is a natural way humans manage stressful situations. But there is a price—the overwhelming experience can linger in your brain as a fragmented memory, continuing to affect you in the long term and sometimes remaining active in your brain for a lifetime.

Your physiological state affects the way events are experienced and remembered. By "physiological state," I mean the regulation of your autonomic nervous system, which controls the internal functions of your body. Your heart rate, blood pressure, digestive system, breath, and other internal functions are "automatically" controlled by your autonomic nervous system. It's also responsible for hardwired survival defenses when you feel threatened; this is the fight-or-flight response, which involves a range of physiological effects. These include chemical changes in your brain and body, which help maximize your ability to survive if you are in a dangerous situation—and also affect the way experiences are processed in your brain as memories.

Instead of moving through to the place in your brain that recognizes the event as taking place in the past, an overwhelming memory can remain "hot" in your brain for decades. Those memories that are left unprocessed can get "bumped" by present-day experiences, the same way you might bump a bruise or open wound. When this happens, instead of just reacting to the present event, you are reacting to hidden pieces of past, unhealed memories. You are, in essence, experiencing a flashback. But if you don't recognize how the past is being ignited, you may just believe you are reacting to the present moment.

When activated, these unresolved memories manifest as physical sensations, emotions, and distorted perceptions of the present moment. In other words, these memories can hijack you in the present, frequently making it difficult to employ typical anger management techniques, like relaxing or controlling your breathing. Because of this, SAFE EMDR isn't an anger management technique per se. Instead, it is a way to access those hidden traumas and potentially bring them to a more adaptive place in your brain, allowing you to react in the present without being overwhelmed by the past.

Anger Protected You

SAFE EMDR has a concept called "The Answer," which will be a key thread throughout this book; it's a simple but deep way of looking at the layers of human experience and behavior, and it's foundational to the SAFE EMDR approach for many reasons. Through the lens of SAFE EMDR, problematic anger is here because it has been (and in some ways, still is) helpful. If you think about early painful experiences as the root of problematic anger, your Answer is how you adapted to those experiences, or how you "learned" from them.

Imagine a small, fiery circle representing an early, painful experience, surrounded by a larger circle, representing all of the ways you have managed to stay away from that painful experience. Those ways become unconscious habits. Habits become what you do best. Problematic anger wasn't something you planned out; it developed naturally because, at one point in your life, it helped, becoming part of your Answer.

But it's also likely true that now, problematic anger is disrupting your life—it may make your relationships more difficult; cause or contribute to health issues; or feel tiring and exhausting to deal with. This book will help you begin to resolve the trauma that lies at the root of your anger so you can approach life differently. With practice of SAFE EMDR, you can learn to live in a calmer, more conscious way.

How to Use This Book

This book is set up in two parts. The first five chapters of this book will help you truly understand the SAFE EMDR principles and the concept of The Answer—which are the safeguards and the foundation of the method—and begin to apply them. The second part of this book discusses the methods and procedures of SAFE EMDR itself.

Keep in mind the first part of the book is practical and not theoretical. You will be invited to experience the foundational principles and practice them. Generally, when you experience something in multiple ways, it can help you learn it more quickly. Mastering the foundational principles of part 1 will help you have a better chance of successfully navigating the work of part 2. The principles in part 1 also help to create safety; this is true for you as a self-help reader and for clinicians who are practicing SAFE EMDR in the therapy office.

You may still be tempted to dive into the second part and skip over the first. No one is here to stop you from doing that. However, it is similar to going on a trip without planning or packing appropriately. Imagine just hopping on an airplane and letting it take you wherever it is going. The plane lands and you get off without any luggage. It turns out that the plane took you to Antarctica and you only have a light jacket. You'll likely be okay; there may be kind people around who will help you find warm clothes, or you could figure out how to get another plane to a warmer place. But wouldn't it be better to plan for the trip prior to taking off?

Part 1: The SAFE EMDR Principles

All of the SAFE EMDR principles are important, and together they support the process of healing. I use the metaphor of a tabletop with four legs supporting it. If you take away one of the legs, the tabletop is not as stable. The four foundational principles of SAFE EMDR work together like four legs on a table; all four are equally important as you begin to create an internal environment for healing problematic anger.

Nonviolence

The first SAFE EMDR principle, which we'll explore in chapter 1, is nonviolence. In this chapter you will be invited to explore and experience ways you fight what is here or try to force things to happen, with both yourself and others. This "extra" effort you expend is not only ineffective, but often pushes the desired outcome further out of reach. Once you grasp the concept of nonviolence—of letting go of the fight with yourself and with life—you may begin to have more awareness of your words, urges, and tendencies, which reflect the extras that you add in. The concept of nonviolence isn't about being nice. It is about recognizing small ways that you are trying to make something happen that is out of your control or not your right to control. Oftentimes when you try to force things, you end up getting the opposite of what you wanted—and feel more frustrated, which fuels chronic anger.

Mindful Awareness

The second foundational SAFE EMDR principle, explored in chapter 2, is mindful awareness. The ability to observe your present-moment experience is essential to successful SAFE EMDR. Really, the only thing you *can* be mindfully aware of is the present moment. This is the opposite of being on autopilot or zoning out. Being mindfully present as you remember the past helps you with both regulation (controlling your emotions) and integration (digesting past experiences). As a result, you will feel more whole as a self.

Compassionate Assumption

Having a compassionate assumption about whatever you experience is the third leg of SAFE EMDR foundational principles, and it's what we'll explore in chapter 3. The assumption is that whatever is here has been helpful or painful. This is a way of viewing yourself and others that is very useful for calming the flames of problematic anger. When you are able to have a compassionate assumption, you are less likely to be tense and upset by people around you. You are also less likely to engage with someone who is activated by the past and not really open to your opinion or resolving anything. Applying a compassionate assumption toward yourself is the most difficult and the most powerful use of this principle.

Healthy Boundaries

Healthy boundaries are the fourth leg of the SAFE EMDR foundational principles, and we'll explore this in chapter 4. By boundaries, I am talking about the healthy recognition of your rights and the rights of others. Having healthy boundaries helps you to ask for what you want and recognize others' right to say yes or no. When you feel violated or taken advantage of by someone else, healthy boundaries help you to recognize how you participated in that experience, which can help you make preventative changes in the future.

Finding Your Answer

The final chapter of the first part of the book is helping you find your Answer, which I mentioned previously. The Answer is an original SAFE EMDR concept that is born out of the foundational principles. In order to most successfully utilize the concept of The Answer, nonviolence, mindful awareness, compassionate assumption, and healthy boundaries all play a part.

Part 2: The Five Steps to Healing Problematic Anger

After experiencing the first half of this book, you will have an opportunity to take steps toward healing the root of problematic anger in part 2. Each of the steps in the second part of the book will build on the others.

For each of these steps, I suggest taking the opportunity to set an intention as you read and experience the corresponding chapter. It is helpful if you have a clear intention; it could be to stay as open as possible to whatever is here, or to read the chapters with an emotional distance to get information. Either of those intentions is fine. You get to decide how you use this book, picking which parts work best for you to navigate either alone or with a SAFE EMDR clinician. You are the only person who can decide what is right for you.

Step One: *Making the Decision to Change*

In this chapter (chapter 6), you'll be invited to explore how much you believe anger is a problem for you, which is the important first step toward healing problematic anger. None of us have the ability to heal or change anyone but ourselves. As you begin to see how problematic anger is your problem and not due to any outside forces, you can make the decision to change it or not.

Step Two: *Embracing Radical Responsibility*

The second step toward healing problematic anger is about embracing radical responsibility. In chapter 7, you will be empowered to explore your role in creating and perpetuating anger-triggering situations. You will be guided to engage in a playful, curious way to discover unconscious agreements and hidden emotional longings.

Step Three: *Connecting the Present to the Past*

In chapter 8, if you are ready and willing to look deeply at the roots of your anger, you will be guided through a process of discovering how pieces of past experiences are still lingering. Exploring how fragmented pieces of the past are in your system can be enlightening and daunting. Depending on the amount of unresolved trauma and current state of your mental health, you may choose to explore this chapter with a qualified mental health professional.

Step Four: *Releasing the Emotional Charge of Past Experiences*

In this chapter, you'll explore the important step of remembering the past in order to heal the present. You will have the option of using some self-help methods to release some of the charge of the past. These exercises are not the same as doing EMDR therapy, but I have found them helpful in my own healing journey. Since these past events are often the hidden root of problematic anger, this is where you have an opportunity to be freed from the grip of past, painful experiences.

Step Five: *A New Peaceful Path*

After releasing the emotional roots of problematic anger, in chapter 10, you have an opportunity to decide what you would like your future to look like. What do you want or need in your life now? What does your life look like without problematic anger? Deciding what you want is like drawing a blueprint for a new home. This chapter and the exercises that accompany it will guide you through the process of designing the life you want to live, not letting someone else do it for you.

Ongoing Guidance and Support

The final chapter of this book, chapter 11, will offer ways to continue the process of healing from destructive anger and unresolved trauma. You will be offered a variety of ways to connect with resources and support. Whether you choose to continue the self-help journey or take a step toward getting professional psychotherapy, this chapter will offer a variety of tools and paths to take.

The path ahead may not be easy, but it is worth it. Avoiding the pain of the past is like putting a bandage on a broken bone; if it gets bumped, it still hurts. The only way out is through. In the next few chapters, I will be offering some protective tools to make the process go as smoothly and comfortably as possible. For additional resources, please explore the free tools available online at http://www.newharbinger.com/54988.

Although it isn't easy, the result of this work can be freedom and peace. Let's begin.

Part 1

Creating a SAFE Path to Healing Anger

Chapter 1

Nonviolence

Do you feel like you keep trying to make a change but nothing changes? Like you keep doing the same thing over and over, even though a part of you knows better? Do you sometimes wonder if you are just "stupid" or "crazy"? Everyone experiences this, and it's all down to our Answer—our strong, adaptive pattern that we have created over our lifetime. Your Answer is like the costume you put over your authentic, shining self. It is both a strength and a limitation. Sometimes, a costume helps us be someone or something that we don't feel we can be on our own. But it can also become restrictive, keeping us from being who we truly are.

The best way to successfully engage with your Answer is to be nonviolent, kind, and patient with yourself. The SAFE EMDR principles are safeguards to help you prepare for the difficult task of looking at your patterns. In this chapter, we'll take a deep dive into the first principle of nonviolence, exploring what it is and how to put it into practice.

The Answer and Nonviolence

Simply put, The Answer is the adaptation you made to maximize safety and connection in your formative years. We all adapt ourselves to either fit in or protect ourselves. There is a reason you adapted; you were either not feeling safe or not feeling connected to the people taking care of you. You were in pain of some kind. These adaptations were created to defend and protect the most vulnerable, authentic part of you.

If you have problematic anger, that anger was likely a helpful adaptation you naturally made at one time. Surprisingly, appreciating how anger was once helpful is more effective than simply trying to force anger to go away.

By approaching our Answer with an accepting, nonviolent tone, we are less likely to offend or defend. If you can imagine there is a part of you who worked hard to get through difficult things, you are talking to that part of you. Imagine a seven-year-old you who was trying to protect a sibling or trying to get approval from critical parents. Whatever the adaptation was for that seven-year-old, it is helpful to appreciate it. You were only seven; you did the best you could in the situation you were in, with the resources you had available. Your reactions to such situations created imprints in your life that became a blueprint for how you are in the world and with others. It is good to begin to question these blueprints now as you see both the ways they helped and how they may be limiting.

Recognizing the "extra" effort that often accompanies your reactions is a part of understanding your Answer. When we are fueled by past situations and using the resources we developed because of painful situations, we are likely to add in something "extra." Here are some examples of extras:

- Extra effort to help someone else feel better.
- Extra effort to not make a mistake.
- Extra effort to achieve something.
- Extra effort to prove something.
- Extra effort to be liked.
- Extra effort to keep the peace.
- Extra effort to make people happy.
- Extra effort to feel important.
- Extra effort to not be seen.
- Extra effort to control things.
- Extra effort to be nice.
- Extra effort to be perfect.

Feel free to write about your favorite extra in your journal.

Nonviolence Is Trauma-Informed

Violence, fear, and loss are the painful roots of anger. As you begin to look at the roots of problematic anger, you are looking at the raw, unprocessed pieces of past experiences that have not yet been moved to the part of your brain that knows the past is over. Those pieces of raw data are like time capsules in your brain. As you access them, your body and brain feel like whatever you're remembering is happening now. That is why you get triggered by some things and not others.

In the EMDR process, you will be invited to intentionally access those fragmented pieces of the past. Practicing nonviolence is a helpful resource when observing those raw pieces of sensory information. If you can observe and allow what is here, those pieces of experience will move to a more adaptive place.

It is also very helpful to remember in such moments that you are just remembering. Whatever you're remembering is not happening now. If you can welcome what is here without trying to make it go away or trying to make something be here that isn't, you will be more successful. If you can be playful with it, that is even better.

Ultimately, even if you notice past memories or habitual negative self-statements that come up, if you have the intention of nonviolence—no longer forcing something to happen that is out of your control or not your right to control—you can see these internal experiences as a part of the memory and simply observe them. You won't waste energy trying to control the uncontrollable, or insist on making sense of things, which makes it harder to understand what's truly going on.

SAFE EMDR and the concept of The Answer have only been taught to EMDR clinicians until now. The concept of nonviolence is one of the most difficult for clinicians to grasp. They are generally helpers and want clients to feel better, so when I tell them that trying to help can sometimes be the most violent thing a therapist can do, they are often surprised. But it's true—because often, clinicians try to help the client make the pain go away instead of allowing it to be there. At times, the clinician may focus on the anger (the trauma-driven behavior) rather than the trauma memory.

The process of healing usually begins with an uncovering, which is an important discovery and sometimes reveals something painful. But that pain is here to be healed, not covered up again. So, instead of trying to make it go away, we are now going toward it with SAFE EMDR. Using the concept of nonviolence, we are allowing and welcoming what is here and providing tools to help you tolerate it. By doing this we allow ourselves to be free from the grasp it has secretly held on us.

Part of healing is the recognition that whatever is here now exists because it wants to move toward a resolution. Those fragmented pieces of the past in your brain are just memories that want to be resolved. To resolve them requires creating a safe environment for the brain to process the experience of the past, without rushing to escape the fear or pain before it has a chance to move.

Trying to Force Change to Happen Doesn't Work

Have you ever planted a tulip? I love to see pink tulips blooming in the spring after a long, cold winter, so I plant lots of them. A tulip starts out as a brown, hard, crusty bulb. In order to have a hope of it blooming, you have to plant the bulb at the proper depth, with its roots facing down, at the right time of year. Once you plant the bulb, it takes time for it to grow. Mother Nature feeds it with rain and sunshine, and in the spring a tulip will finally push through the dirt and bloom.

What if you tried to *force* the tulip to bloom? Imagine taking a tulip bulb, sticking it in the ground, and then simply yelling at it to grow. Imagine comparing it to the other tulips and telling it how ugly it is or shaming the bulb for not blooming. How do you think that would go?

The principle of nonviolence is similar to planting a tulip. It recognizes the importance of establishing nourishing conditions that allow transformation to happen. Transformation can never be forced; you can't force yourself or anyone else to change. However, you can have an intention to allow positive transformation to happen and set the stage for it to unfold. Understanding and applying the foundational principle of nonviolence is about creating the conditions for positive change without trying to force it.

When I talk about nonviolence, I am referring to both how you relate to others and to yourself. If you want to heal problematic anger, you first need to realize the damage that anger toward yourself or others creates. In many cases, our anger is rewarded, which can create a vicious cycle that ultimately leads to further intensified anger reactions. Once you can really see and believe that chronic anger is damaging, you have an opportunity to heal.

As we explore the problem with chronic anger as a form of violence, keep in mind that the intention is to motivate change, not to make you feel shame or guilt. The past is over, but the present and future offer you an opportunity to learn and grow.

Anger Toward Others Makes Things Worse

Have you ever heard any professional recommend that parents yell at their kids? Most professionals don't, and for good reason. In many cases, yelling often stops an unwanted behavior. This typically reinforces parents' belief in the tactic, because it appears to be effective—even if it's also likely to cause other forms of damage, like fear or resentment on the part of the child.

This cycle presents the biggest problem. Violence appears to be effective in the short term, but the long-term result is damage to the parent's relationship with the child, and the child's sense of emotional security and safety with others. The child may also develop other unwanted emotions or behaviors, which can present covertly, rather than overtly. A natural result may be long-term passive-aggressive or procrastination behaviors.

Listed below are some unwanted, longer-term effects of using violence toward children or anyone you have power over, like people you supervise at work or other situations:

- The child is more likely to use violence toward others.
- The child learns to lie.
- The child feels like a bad person and has low self-esteem.
- The child is afraid of you.
- The child learns to be passive aggressive, finding small ways to get back at you like avoiding tasks or feigning obedience.
- The child doesn't feel safe.

When you use violence toward children, there is a chance they will feel overpowered and go into a state of collapse, stopping all behavior. The other option is they go into a state of fight or flight, which may escalate until they go into a state of collapse or helplessness. Either way, the child is in a trauma response.

If you are feeling shame or guilt while reading this, I strongly encourage you to keep reading. The only useful thing about guilt and shame is to motivate you to change your behavior; otherwise it just fuels the problem of anger. If there is a better way, are you interested in learning more about it?

A Case Example

Fourteen-year-old James was brought into therapy by his mother. She stated that she and her husband were angry and frustrated by James's behavior, and were at the end of their rope. James's mother reported that he was failing eighth grade, not because he wasn't capable of doing the work, but because he refused to. The school created a behavior plan for him, but he was often sent to detention for not completing his work. James's mother had tried everything from monitoring his assignments online to even doing the homework for him, only to later find it wadded up in the bottom of his locker. She reported that his room was empty—no games or screens, only his bed—and that he was grounded from seeing his friends.

When working with children and teens, I am always interested in the parents' view and history. James's parents were both hard-working people who valued productivity. They both grew up in lower-middle-class homes and worked hard to create a comfortable life for their children. They both had strong beliefs about right and wrong and didn't understand why their son was being so stubborn.

James was receiving extreme pressure and lots of anger from his parents and school officials. As I sat across from James in my office, I noticed that he was slumped in his chair, arms crossed. As his therapist, I decided to tell him the truth. I said, "I have a problem." This seemed to get his attention, and for the first time he looked at me. I said, "It seems like everyone is pressuring you to do something." He still said nothing, but was clearly engaged. I continued, "So the problem is, I'm guessing that if I start asking you questions, you are going to feel like I'm doing the same thing, pressuring you. So I don't know what to do." He was very interested at this point, and we sat for a long moment looking at each other.

I got out of my chair and sat on the floor with my feet curled under me. I put my head down and covered my head with a large cowl from my sweater, looking like a turtle inside the shell. I stayed there for what felt like a long time, with no idea what would happen. Finally, James got out of his chair, then took the drumstick from my floor drum and peeked under my collar. We were both sitting on the floor and he started talking. From that moment on, he knew I understood. James's parents' anger was creating such a force that he had to turn into a rock. The more pressure they put on him, the more solid the rock became.

Because James finally had an adult who understood, he opened up to me. We were able to use EMDR therapy on his memories of feeling like he didn't measure up to his younger, high-achieving brother and some memories of being bullied at school. James was doing his part to heal and really wanted to do better.

I knew that the most difficult part of this process would be convincing his parents that their angry, punitive approach was not only not working but making the situation much worse. His parents didn't bring him into therapy to hear that they needed to change. I met with James's mother and asked her, "On a scale of 0 to 10, how motivated are you to have James do better in school?" She quickly answered, "Very, 10." Then I asked her, "On a scale of 0 to 10, how uncomfortable are you willing to be for that to happen?" She hesitated on that one, but answered "Ten." I then explained my theory of why James was resisting doing what they wanted and how the more pressure they put on him, the more he adapted by becoming like a rock. I also explained that there is a difference between punishment and discipline. I asked her if what they were currently doing was making things worse, would she be open to trying something very different? She said yes. I recommended giving him back all of his things and ungrounding him, as well as stopping both the monitoring of his school work and the school behavior plan. She knew that James's father wouldn't like the recommendations, but she was committed to helping her son. We discussed how to present this as an experiment.

I am aware of how difficult it can be to change a pattern, and I give James's parents so much credit for making a difficult change. In a few weeks, James and his mother came back into my office and reported he was getting B's. Taking off the pressure allowed James to have freedom of choice.

James's case is a great example of the SAFE concept of The Answer and the power of nonviolence. Viewed in isolation, James's behavior seemed like disobedience. Viewed in context, James was adapting to his environment, becoming a rock to withstand the pressure of his parents' anger and punishment. His parents were also doing what they did best, trying hard to make things happen. When we are stuck and things just get worse the harder we try, it is likely the result of our Answer being there, trying to help but actually making things worse. But because it is what we do best, we keep doing it anyway.

If we feel justified in our anger, we often conclude that there is something wrong with the world or other people and fail to look at ourselves. But as with James, that judgment and anger were likely the true cause of the problem. Understanding how your anger and judgment can exacerbate an outside problem is a tough concept to grasp. This is especially the case if your early environment included strict religious rules or authoritarian values, which can reinforce the belief that people deserve your anger. But as I often say to parents, "Just because what you are doing is making things worse, doesn't mean you should keep doing it."

How might this principle be at work in your own life? Are there situations or people in your life that you're approaching with force—making things worse, not better? Trying to make things happen with force will always create a counterforce of some kind. It is difficult to look at ourselves, and more difficult to change. The first step is recognizing that anger and judgment are not working and are likely making your life and the lives of your loved ones worse. If you can take that step, it is a huge leap!

The next step is to cultivate curiosity about what's happening, so you can set the stage to change it. Curiosity is the opposite of judgment. If you are in a state of curiosity, it is impossible to be in a state of judgment. A nonjudgmental, curious frame of mind about your experience is crucial for maintaining a nonviolent stance toward it, yourself, and others. Ironically, the first step to changing your anger is to be curious about it.

If you want to start being less angry and more nonviolent, practice is key. The following exercise is meant to help you shift from judgment and anger to curiosity and wonder. It is best to practice this when you are not actually experiencing intense anger or judgment so your brain can begin to make that shift more gradually. I learned about the power of making the "Hmm" sound from my friends and teachers Katie and Gay Hendricks, authors of *Conscious Loving* and many other wonderful books. It turns out you cannot make the sound "Hmm" and be judgmental at the same time. The "Hmm" sound helps to activate curiosity, which is the opposite of judgment.

EXERCISE: Curiosity Toward Others

1. I invite you to bring up a time when you wanted someone to do something and they didn't do it. Maybe your partner disappointed you, your child didn't follow the rules, or a coworker didn't pull their weight; something recent but not too disturbing. As you bring up that experience, I invite you to notice your judgment toward the other person. Notice your thoughts that may sound something like this: "She is so lazy." "He is disrespectful." "She is irresponsible." Whatever your actual judgment is, just notice that.
2. Now I would like to invite you to notice what you are experiencing in your body. Where are you feeling tension? If you would like, write down a description of the body sensation.
3. Now I would like to invite you to intentionally try to be curious about that person. It helps to start off with making a "hmm" sound. "Hmm, I wonder if there is a really good reason for that person's behavior?" "Hmm, I wonder, if I really understood what was going on for that person, would I have a different reaction?"
4. Now, continue to make the "hmm" sound out loud and notice the area of your body where you previously felt tension. Has it changed?

Take some time to practice this activity at least a few times over the next several days. Make a note of the changes you see.

Applying Nonviolence to Yourself

When I was in elementary school, once a year we had a "Fun Night." There were games in every classroom and we won prizes for catching a "fish" with a clothespin we threw over a blanket. One of the prizes was a finger trap—a woven device with two open ends for you to stick your fingers in. When you put opposite fingers in each end and pulled, the device became tighter. The harder you tried to pull your fingers out, the tighter it got. It was only when you relaxed and pushed your fingers into the device that you could release the toy. The finger trap is a great metaphor for nonviolence and how it applies to anger or anything else you want to change about yourself. The first step out is inward.

With problematic anger or any other issue, acknowledging and accepting the current state is a necessary first step. If you get mad at yourself for getting angry, it is similar to pouring fuel on a flame.

Often it's easier to have compassion for other people than for yourself. But applying the concept of nonviolence to your own healing path is crucial in SAFE EMDR. Often people believe that they can "just stop" being angry by willing themselves to do so. This rarely works. And when people try forcing themselves to change and fail, they often end up frustrated and disappointed in themselves. This frustration and disappointment fuel the anger further, instead of healing it.

Remember the tulips from earlier in this chapter? It's important to recognize that you cannot force yourself to change. Transformation only happens by setting the conditions for the change to happen. And approaching yourself with nonviolence is a crucial part of those conditions.

Why Applying Nonviolence to Yourself Will Be Helpful

Again, the first half of this book is what we call the "preparation phase" of SAFE EMDR. Here, you are doing the initial work to make getting to the root memories easier. So what I am recommending isn't just fluffy, therapy stuff. You are laying down the foundation for the next phase of your healing. Just as in building a house, the foundation is important to the safety of the structure. By having the intention of being nonviolent toward yourself, you are beginning to change your brain.

Your brain is a very efficient organ that likes habits. Most thoughts and behaviors—including the ones that feed your chronic anger—are on autopilot because that is what our brain is geared toward: efficiency. Your brain doesn't really care if what you are doing is good for you or bad for you; it's just following orders.

You probably have habitual thought patterns of beating yourself up and judging yourself harshly. Those habits likely started when you were very young. In this book, you will begin to understand how being hard on yourself was likely helpful as a child. Perhaps when you were a kid, your parents or others acted in hurtful ways toward you. If so, it may have been much easier to believe that you were the problem. As a child, you need your parents to survive, and you trust that your parents have authority and wisdom. It could be really scary for a child to think there is something wrong with their parents. What's more, kids are developmentally disposed to believe things happen because of them. They may not know enough about the way the world works to understand context and other factors, or the responsibilities of adults.

So what do I mean by practicing nonviolence with yourself? Nonviolence starts with the intention to be kinder and more compassionate with yourself. It involves understanding yourself nonjudgmentally, including the conditions that have shaped your behavior. When you begin to do this, you are changing the biology of your brain as well as its habitual pathways. Compassion, kindness, and appreciation are emotions that create heart rate coherence—regulation in the patterns of your heartbeat—which is associated with increased health and longevity (McCraty 2017). In addition, following these practices trains your brain to recognize that you are safe, which is a physiological sense that is very important as you begin to work with the unprocessed, painful memories that fuel problematic anger. Cultivating nonviolence toward yourself prior to addressing past traumas will help the process go more smoothly. You'll also be able to observe shame and guilt as part of your difficult memories, rather than as your current reality.

Another benefit of practicing self-directed nonviolence is the effect it has on the healing process. Again, at the root of problematic anger are memories that are physiologically stored in your brain and have not had an opportunity to move through your system. Research has shown that those memories are fragments of earlier, overwhelming experiences (Kearney and Lanius 2022). To integrate these memories and heal from them, you must foster a sense of safety. Think about what you needed as a child when those painful events were happening. Maybe it was kindness, understanding, language to really understand what you were experiencing, or forgiveness. Those are the qualities that define the safe environment we want to create now. We don't want to try to force; judgment and anger will only serve to keep you stuck in the past. Nonviolence, allowing and welcoming whatever is here, and knowing it is just a memory, will pave the way for true healing.

The following exercise will allow you to begin building this healing environment of nonjudgmental, curious understanding.

EXERCISE: Curiosity with Yourself

I'd like to invite you to bring up a recent, mild time that you had a judgment about yourself. Don't make it a big thing, just a time that you had critical thoughts about yourself. Think about your favorite, habitual way you scold yourself with your thoughts. It might be something like:

- "How could I be so stupid?"
- "When will I ever learn?"
- "I'm a piece of crap."
- "What the ________ (heck) is wrong with you?"
- "I hate myself."
- "Dumb ________ (fill in the expletive).
- Any other harsh thought you tell yourself.

Notice if your tendency is to use the word "I" or "You" when you are mentally beating yourself up. "You" can indicate you are repeating what someone else told you.

Notice what you are experiencing in your body. Notice any tension or tightness. Now I would like to invite you to intentionally activate curiosity toward being more nonviolent with yourself. It might sound something like this:

- "Hmm, I wonder if this thing I keep telling myself has been helpful."
- "Hmm, I wonder if I could allow myself to be human, make mistakes, AND be kind to myself?"
- "Hmm, I wonder if being kinder to myself would help me heal?"

Repeat the "Hmm" curiosity statement several times and notice any shift in your body. You might also try practicing this curious, nonjudgmental approach the next time you find yourself feeling angry with yourself in day-to-day life. See if you can pause, the next time a self-punishing thought comes up, and notice what you're telling yourself and how you feel in your body. And see if stopping to notice this, without judgment, helps open a door for you to behave differently than your anger or first instincts tell you to behave.

Practicing Change

Keep in mind that change requires practice. If after reading this chapter you are feeling motivated to take a more nonviolent path, then keep taking the next step: noticing your automatic negative thoughts about yourself and others. And know that because the pathways that lead you to automatic negative thoughts are well-worn ones, they will continue to happen. Just noticing those negative reactions when they happen, having that little bit of awareness, is progress. It opens the opportunity to replace that negative judgment with something more accepting or kind. For example:

> "How could I be so stupid?" can be replaced with "It's okay to make mistakes."

> "People are idiots" can be replaced with "We are all doing the best we can."

As you make that shift, it is helpful to also notice if something shifts in your physical body. Are you feeling less tension?

In addition to the negative thought reactions, you can begin to notice when you are trying to force change to happen. You will notice that by noticing the feelings of frustration and impatience that might arise. At those times, the practice will be accepting what is here and breathing into those emotions. Every time you are able to recognize frustration and impatience and breathe into it, you are changing the pathways in your brain to more peaceful ones.

Chapter 2

The Power of the Present Moment

It was day three of my first ten-day silent meditation retreat. I had no experience meditating. I had found the retreat through a Google search and simply registered to attend. The meditation is called Vipassana, a word that means "seeing things as they really are." It is also known as mindfulness meditation or insight meditation.

The retreat was intense. As participants, we meditated for nine-plus hours a day. The meditators observe noble silence and vow to have no communication with other meditators, verbal or otherwise. When you arrive at the meditation center you voluntarily hand over your phone and car keys if you have them. There is nothing to distract yourself—no television, music, books, or snacks. There are two meals a day, breakfast at 6:30 a.m. and lunch at 11:00 a.m. All of the tools we use to distract from the present moment are gone.

The first three days were spent focusing on the breath going in and out, with the goal of calming the mind. On day four we learned the Vipassana meditation method. In simple terms, it consists of noticing your body sensations inch by inch from your head to your toes and then back up. We remained silent the entire ten days, except for five-minute opportunities to ask the teacher any questions we had about the method. After an hour-long group meditation, I had a chance to talk to the teacher. I told him I noticed that after meditating for a while, my body began slightly swaying to the beat of my heart. The teacher said he noticed that I did that after about forty minutes of sitting. Since there were forty to fifty meditation students and one teacher, I was impressed that he'd noticed. He wondered if the swaying was a way to distract myself or stay away from something. I told him that I could try to stop myself from swaying and he suggested that I try that.

In the next group session, I noticed when my body started to sway and stopped it. After a few minutes, my body became hot and I felt like my entire torso was on fire; the heat sensation spread to my limbs and I sat in a whole-body inferno for the rest of the meditation time. This lasted fifteen to twenty minutes at the end of an hour-long sit, but to me, it felt like an eternity. I understood that I was previously swaying my body to stay away from this sensation.

After the meditation ended, I got up—and I began to notice automatic judgmental thoughts. I decided to observe those thoughts, just as I had the body sensations. I went to the cafeteria for lunch and noticed an automatic judgment toward a person sitting across from me. She sneezed and I thought to myself, "Really, you have to choose to sit right across from me and sneeze? This process is hard enough without getting a cold!"

I decided to play with my angry view and I looked around to see if I could find something to be irritated about with everyone I looked at. A very kind-looking woman walked into the cafeteria and I thought, "Hello, Miss Always Last in Line." As I looked around, I could find something to be irritated about with every person I saw, with the exception of one woman, who looked to be eight months pregnant. As I saw the pregnant woman, I could feel nothing but compassion and admiration for her. A ten-day silent meditation retreat is very difficult and I could not imagine completing the retreat while being so pregnant. This experience gave me a new perspective on my anger and I was able to see the true root of anger was in me. I understood that my anger was mine, in me, and about no one or nothing outside of me.

This experience revealed how I used busyness to avoid confronting difficult emotions and memories. I'm really good at projects, manifesting my ideas, planning my next adventure, and in general, "doing." This has allowed me to achieve many good things, but has also shielded me from certain deeper feelings and experiences. And it wasn't until that ten-day silent retreat that I could access these remnants of the past lying latent in my nervous system. Prior to that, I could only access my anger when it was triggered by something and I had an angry response, which increased the likelihood of more outbursts in the future.

Vipassana is a powerful and deep type of meditation. One thing it teaches is how we may be reacting to body sensations, which combine with our thoughts to create strong habit patterns.

Am I recommending that you attend a ten-day silent meditation retreat to heal your chronic anger? Yes. However, I am aware that most people do not have the interest or motivation to do that. So in this chapter, I offer you some small ways to increase your present-moment awareness—ways to begin developing a mind-body connection and a mindful awareness of your experience in the present moment—as a way to express anger and other emotions differently than you otherwise might.

There is a misconception in our society that things outside of ourselves have the power to make us angry. It's true that anger, like any feeling, can be a response to conditions. But it's also true that it's an experience *within* us, and as such, we have a degree of control over how we react to it and express it. If anger is a problem in your life, it is not about anyone but you, and that is the good news. If you are ultimately responsible for your anger, you also have the power to change it.

Mind-Body Connection

Is there any doubt that the mind-body connection exists? If you wonder, you may want to try a little self-experiment. Think about eating your favorite food. Maybe you are like me and love to eat pizza. As you remember the last time you ate a really good piece of pizza or your favorite food, what do you notice? Does an image of a pizza come to mind? Maybe you imagine the sight of the glistening, melted cheese, cooked to perfection. You may also remember the taste and the texture of the pizza—the salty cheese, the zesty tomato, the savory herbs. As you recall this in your mind, what do you notice in your body? Maybe you notice a feeling of happiness. Maybe that happiness manifests as a light, airy feeling in your chest and an open tingling that expands outward as you take in a breath. You may also notice your saliva in your mouth and feel the urge to swallow. Maybe you think of baking a pizza in the future or going to your favorite pizza joint.

As this exercise reveals, just by activating a memory, we have set off a stream of psychobiological events and chemical reactions. Feeling and observing this connection can be amazing.

However, the mind-body connection can also be a source of suffering. When the interaction between the mind and the body is informed by something painful from the past, the connection can build a well-worn neural highway that keeps the pain of the past events ignited. Each event that lights the fire of the past adds more logs and heat. Because the source of our pain is hidden, this makes it more likely that we will blame the external world for our reaction.

You may hear people who are angry about the government, the state of the world, factory farms, or the behavior of a friend or neighbor. Though all of these things are real, it is unlikely that the angry person will look inside and see how earlier, unprocessed events and their own history of reactivity may be the actual source of the suffering, not the external events. Ultimately, the only thing we can control is ourselves, although that is a very difficult task!

Noticing Breath Experiment

Your breath is a constant presence and a wonderful tool for helping you come to the present moment. If you are caught up in thoughts, emotions, memories, or any other way the past manifests, your breath can help.

1. Start by setting a timer for five minutes. You can gradually make it longer as you practice this skill.
2. Close your eyes and begin to notice your breath without trying to change it.
3. Notice a spot under your nose and focus on your breath coming in and going out.

4. Notice how the breath is slightly cooler coming in and warmer going out.
5. You may notice thoughts or other things and lose your awareness of your breath. Smile and gently bring your focus back to that spot below your nostrils. Notice the sensation of the breath coming in and going out.

Practicing this exercise for a few minutes each day can help you develop a useful tool to calm your mind.

Fighting Against the Present Moment

Whatever is here is here. Our reaction to the truth of any moment is what creates suffering. There is great wisdom in the serenity prayer: "God, grant me the serenity to accept the things I cannot change, the courage to change the things I can, and the wisdom to know the difference." The Buddhists also recognize three "poisons" or negative states of mind that create most of our problems: Craving (or Greed), Hatred (or Anger), and Delusion (or Ignorance). To put that into practical terms, if you can accept what is here in the present moment without hating it, craving something different, or trying to ignore it, that's the first step. The second step is recognizing any way you played a part in the "undesirable" present moment, then taking steps to make the changes you can make. Doing this will help you increase wisdom and decrease suffering. Just to be clear, this is a lofty goal, but it is possible.

The SAFE EMDR concept of The Answer is about finding what is out of balance. The Answer is the way we all naturally adapt to our unique life circumstances so as to maximize safety and connection. It will be revealed in our physical bodies, automatic habits, strengths, and how we respond when we are under stress. In chapter 5, you will be guided through the process of discovering your unique Answer. But it's also important to know how the SAFE EMDR principle of mindful awareness relates to The Answer.

Our physical bodies will always reveal what we are avoiding or doing in excess. Even as tiny babies, we begin storing somatic memories. Our physical bodies are impersonal, faithful servants. The psychobiological reaction happens instantly and without discrimination. As we try to avoid the pain of the present moment, we cut off awareness of parts of ourselves. We constrict and contort our bodies to avoid the physical sensation that goes along with the discomfort. This is not a conscious choice but more of an adaptation, especially when we are very young and have few coping strategies. This adaptation then becomes a habitual way of responding to circumstances we face in the world.

These adaptations and responses are not something we can think our way through. The only answer is to allow, with curiosity, the body to move toward healing. The paradox is that the more we try to make our somatic reactions go away, the more they return, usually with more intensity than the last time.

Until we can turn toward the truth of the moment, we remain in the cycle of suffering. We are constantly searching for a way to avoid direct contact with the truth. We can go toward the truth by leaning into the pain of the past as it is surfacing in the present moment. As we do this, we are facing the ghosts and realizing they are just an illusion. We are letting go of the ways we are creating our own suffering. Then we are on the path to healing problematic anger.

Our human system is built to survive and connect, and we feel overwhelmed if our survival or connection is threatened, so we adapt. This adaptation is an attempt to maximize safety and connection, and it works. The fact that it has worked is now a part of the problem. It became a habit, and the beauty of a habit is it happens automatically, outside of our conscious awareness. For that reason, increasing awareness of how we are constricting or contracting is the first step.

How do you increase awareness? You begin by observing what you are currently doing. What is it you do best? Ironically, you can discover this by looking at what you complain about the most. Your strength is hidden in your most frequent behaviors that you would like to stop doing.

Here are some possible examples:

Good at thinking	"I worry too much"
Good at being productive	"No one helps me"
Good at reading emotions	"I try to make people happy"
Good at helping/protecting people	"People take advantage of me"

In the world of psychotherapy, we call this the "Presenting Problem." The Presenting Problem is the issue that brings the client to therapy, whether it's a specific difficulty or a persistent yearning for something. What if understanding and even appreciating the "problem" would actually help expedite the process of eradicating it? And when I say "eradicating," I mean having an array of other options and a feeling of being free. If that problem has persisted for quite a while, it is unlikely to ever completely go away, and we really don't want that to happen. Especially if it is your strength and has served you well to maximize safety and connection. The best scenario is for our "problem" to willingly yield to other options, offering flexibility and a variety of choices.

In the case of anger, since it is a part of our built-in human survival system, you will not lose it if you heal the early wounds that are fueling it. You will only lose the problematic anger that is an overreaction to the present situation, because its fuel source (early unhealed wounds) will no longer be feeding the flame.

If avoiding pain and discomfort only increases that pain and discomfort, and if our problems are actually the things we do best, then what? Are we just doomed to misery? Why would we want to have more awareness of painful things? Is it just to punish ourselves for some masochistic reason? Absolutely not.

Going toward the pain of the past is different than intentionally creating pain for ourselves. Everyone is looking for happiness and freedom, but if our attempts to stay away from pain create more of it and make it worse, maybe we should consider a different path. The SAFE EMDR approach helps you get through the pain in the least painful way possible by applying its principles, concepts, and methods appropriately.

How Does Present-Moment Mindfulness Help Heal Anger?

Chronic anger creates strong habits of judgment and tension. Something happens and we react. At that moment of reaction, awareness of bodily sensations or the influence of past experiences is diminished. It just happens and you are angry. Expanding awareness is the first step to healing problematic anger. So how does awareness help? It isn't just being aware that you are angry; that's easy. When you are just aware of being angry, you are also strengthening the anger response and the anger pathways in your brain. To change the pattern, you need to change the awareness. Every anger reaction has a body sensation that goes along with it. Since it is a habit, a well-worn neural pathway in your brain, the body sensation will likely be in the same area most of the time.

To begin to recognize your mind-body pattern, I would like to invite you to try this experiment:

Body Sensation Experiment

1. Bring to mind a recent time when you felt mildly angry.
2. As you bring that to mind, notice any place you are feeling tension and tightness in your body. Notice your shoulders, abdominal muscles, jaw, neck, lower back, or any other area you feel tension. (Remember, your head is a part of your body.)
3. Does this tension feel familiar to you? Does it feel like a habitual pattern?
4. Now shift to something good that happened lately. Maybe an encounter with a good friend, a fun time with family, or a time that was really enjoyable. Notice what changes in your body. How did the sensation change?

Beginning to notice your body sensation is a very helpful way to increase awareness. It will also be useful to help de-escalate anger, which I'll discuss more later. The first step is getting used to noticing that there is a body sensation for every thought. By observing the sensation, you are interrupting an old pattern. The mind-body connection is real and powerful. If you had difficulty with the last experiment, I'd like to offer another one.

Say the word "No" several times. Notice what you are feeling in your body. Now say the word "Yes" several times and notice what changes.

If you noticed nothing at all with either experiment, don't worry. For some people, it has been very helpful to not notice body sensations. This is an example of The Answer. Sometimes it is really helpful not to notice body sensations and to spend time thinking about things instead. So if that is the case for you, try to appreciate how it was to not notice your body. That appreciation may also begin to change the pattern.

Mindfulness Is Not Relaxation

At the Personal Transformation Institute (PTI), we start our training events and meetings with present-moment mindfulness. I have found that starting a meeting with the invitation to be present changes the tone and feeling of that meeting. People are less distracted, they talk more slowly, and the words they say seem to have more aliveness. But present-moment mindfulness is not relaxation—there is a big difference. Many relaxation techniques use mindfulness as a tool, but that is different from the present-moment mindfulness in SAFE EMDR. However, practicing nonjudgmental observation of what is here does often result in less tension and more relaxation.

The difference is, when you are doing a relaxation exercise, the goal is to help yourself relax. With present-moment mindfulness, we are just exploring what is here, without trying to change it. With EMDR, we want to practice allowing what is here to be here, which is an important skill to have as you access the early, stuck pieces of memories. In the previous chapter I talked about the principle of nonviolence. Keeping that concept in mind as you practice present-moment mindfulness will help you to be open to whatever is here, without trying to force or change it.

Present-moment awareness is one of the most difficult things for people to understand and practice. So many people are used to trying to make things happen and they miss the opportunity to experience what is here first! The paradox is, it does change as we explore and observe what is here in an open and curious way. Because you are open and curious about what is here instead of trying to change the experience, you are interrupting the pattern.

EXERCISE: Mindfulness

I recommend reading each question below and taking time to notice your experience before moving on to the next step. It may also be helpful to write your answers in a journal.

1. I'd like to invite you to close your eyes and notice any place in your body where you feel tension or tightness. Take a moment to do that now if you wish.
2. As you focus on that tension or tightness, notice if the sensation feels familiar to you.
3. If that tension or tightness could speak, what would it be saying?
4. As you notice those words, or even silence, does an earlier time come to mind when those words, or lack thereof, were trying to help you?
5. Is there a way that you can give yourself sincere appreciation for how you adapted to your circumstances?

Keeping One Foot in the Present

As you practice present-moment awareness, both in the abstract and in relation to your experiences of anger, you might notice old memories arising. Successful EMDR processing also requires that you access the old memories that fuel your experience of anger—while being present. If you have no sense of being rooted in the present moment as you access an old memory, it is called a flashback. You are too much in the past and not enough in the present. If flashbacks worked to move difficult memories to a more adaptive place in the brain, we would not need EMDR therapy. The reason flashbacks do not result in any resolution is there is no present-moment awareness. The memory takes the old pathway in the brain, over and over again, resulting in a stronger reaction. The purpose of any form of EMDR is to lessen the emotional reaction of a memory.

Remember, the root memories relating to problematic anger are stored in your brain as fragments of raw emotional and sensory information. When the memory happened, it was so overwhelming that your brain couldn't handle it. It is likely that a survival instinct kicked in, as the human system's number one job is survival. When survival instincts are triggered, the brain's memory-processing function can shut down, leaving the memory fragmented and in raw form. When that raw memory is activated, it feels like it is happening now (Kearney et al. 2023).

With SAFE EMDR, we practice mindful awareness of the present moment to help change the pathway of the brain. Imagine a wild river raging and how easily you could be swept up in it. Now imagine building a water management system that harnesses the river's power. This system still allows it to flow but slows and alters its course. By practicing mindful awareness, we are creating a system to change the flow of those memories.

A Case Example

Anna was a bright, beautiful woman who came into therapy to get help with anger outbursts. Anna had experienced sexual and physical abuse by both parents, starting around age three and continuing until she left the house at age eighteen. In the course of her life, Anna became really good at cutting off from her physical experience.

In the past, dissociation helped her cope with the abuse, allowing her to survive while remaining sufficiently psychologically intact. Now, in Anna's adult life, dissociation from her physical experience was a problem. In order to resolve her anger outbursts and effectively reprocess her traumatic memories, Anna had to spend some time practicing mindful awareness—the opposite of dissociation.

We spent much of treatment helping her prepare to face and resolve some of the most difficult memories of her childhood. As she was reprocessing one very disturbing experience, she reported an intense body sensation, which persisted through several sets of bilateral eye movements. She appeared to be stuck in the process. I suggested, "Can you welcome that body sensation?" Anna looked at me with wide eyes and said, "Welcome this?!" I said, "Yes." She said, "I can try." We continued the reprocessing, and the sensation began to lessen and eventually subsided.

By welcoming the thing she had been avoiding and hating for so many years, Anna was able to create enough safety in her system to digest that horrific memory. From there, she was able to get a lot of benefits from SAFE EMDR. As a result, she was able to get off of the antidepressant and mood stabilizers she had been on for many years. This all helped her to feel less numb and more alive. She ended therapy with significantly fewer anger outbursts.

Relational Mindfulness Experiment

It can be very helpful for you to practice being present and mindful with another person. In this exercise, I would like to invite you to activate sincere curiosity about your experience. Try to let yourself be surprised by what you notice. If you find yourself trying to think of what to notice next as your partner is talking, report that. Try to be as honest as possible while remaining appropriate and kind.

1. Two people sit or stand facing each other.
2. One person starts and states anything they are noticing.

3. From then on, you each take turns saying, "Hearing that, I'm noticing..."

Just practicing noticing your experience can be a powerful way of practicing mindful awareness.

What Mindfulness and Emotional Regulation Makes Possible

Increasing your ability to be mindful about your present-moment experience is a powerful way to calm emotional reactivity. It could also make you healthier. What if you found out that emotional distress could negatively impact your health, work, relationships, or even your golf game? What if being calm and relaxed could help heal your body, your mind, relationships at work and at home, or even take strokes off of your golf game?

This book is geared toward people who are having issues with anger, but problematic anger is also a problem with emotional regulation. Emotional regulation is the ability to recognize emotions and use skills to alter those emotions. Emotional regulation is a factor in experiences like excess worry, fear, anxiety, depression, addiction, and any number of other forms of psychological and physiological pain, all of which can be eased or exacerbated by emotional regulation or lack of it.

If this is true, which research shows it is, why isn't emotional regulation the top skill taught at home, school, and work? Why don't we include mindfulness practices in preschool, at the workplace, in prisons and hospitals? I don't have the answer for why we don't, but I do have some evidence to back up why we should.

The short version is this: emotional dysregulation creates tension, tension creates restriction, restriction creates stagnation, stagnation creates pain and illness. Pain and illness create unhappiness, and unhappiness is shared with others, whether you recognize it or not. Even if the result of your unhappiness is self-isolation, there is someone out there missing you or missing out on receiving the gifts you have to offer your family, community, or the world.

On the other hand, emotional regulation creates relaxation, relaxation creates flow, flow creates expansion, expansion creates happiness and freedom. When you are happy and free, you share it with others, whether you recognize it or not. Even if the result of you being free and happy is to go be alone and meditate in a cave, the world is better because of the positive energy you are generating.

In short, practicing mindful awareness of your present-moment experience will be very helpful as you begin the eye movement, reprocessing part of SAFE EMDR. It will also help you expand your ability to own and manage your emotional reactions.

I encourage you to continue practicing the Noticing Breath Experiment and the Relational Mindfulness Experiment exercises over the next few weeks. The more you can make mindful awareness a part of your emotional regulation and your life, the more benefit you'll receive—in chapter 3 and beyond.

Chapter 3

Compassionate Assumption for Yourself and Others

I went to the grocery store with my six-year-old son. We were buying supplies to make cookies, feeling happy and excited to bake together. We arrived at the checkout line and put the ingredients on the belt. The cashier began ringing up the items without looking up or greeting us. After scanning an item, she threw it into the bag. I paid for the groceries, and as I was walking away with my son, I said to him, "Well, she wasn't very nice." From my view, the cashier was being rude to us. My son looked up at me and said, "She probably just lost her dog." We'd lost our pet not too long ago. As he shared his view, my heart melted for her. My son had a compassionate assumption about the cashier.

The stories we tell ourselves about the events in our world are viewed through the lens of our past experiences. Have you ever worn a pair of sunglasses where, when you put them on, everything appears to be a different color? If you don't recognize the influence of the glasses, you think it is reality. You have no idea that the glasses are the reason everything looks different. The same applies to how we interpret experiences in life. When something happens, we tell ourselves a story about it, one that usually features aspects of our past experiences. For example, my experience of the cashier being rude differed from my son's experience of her potential sadness. We both had a different story about it. I grew up the youngest of ten children, seven of whom were female. Past experiences of females being mean to me influenced my perception. In my son's life, his experience was colored by the recent loss of a precious pet dog. If we would have interviewed other customers who interacted with the cashier, we would have likely gotten a different interpretation from each person, all reflecting on something about their past.

Some of you may hear the word "compassion" and think I am suggesting this because it's simply the "nice" thing to do. I want to be clear that anything I suggest in this book—including having a compassionate assumption—is to help free you from problematic anger and bring you healing. The goal is not to be "good," but to be free.

The SAFE EMDR principle of compassionate assumption recognizes that we are all living with ghosts of our past experiences that are still here, coloring our view of ourselves and the world. In addition, we assume that whatever is here right now—especially things that appear to be "overreactions" or "crazy" behavior—is here because that person has lived through some difficult things that would inspire compassion in us if we knew their whole story.

A Compassionate Assumption Is Trauma-Informed

As I stated earlier, the four principles of SAFE EMDR work together to create a SAFE foundation, also known by mental health professionals as a "trauma-informed" approach. When you hear the word "trauma," you might think about physical trauma, war experiences, or other extreme experiences. When I use the term "trauma," I am talking about anything that was too overwhelming for your system to manage. It is any experience that your brain could not completely digest, leaving remnants of it in your brainstem. When triggered by a similar present situation, the raw memory resurfaces, feeling like it's happening in the present moment. We don't recognize how the fuel of the past has contributed to an overreaction to the present. So as we begin the EMDR healing process, having an assumption that an early, unprocessed experience is fueling the present is helpful. If you are feeling a high level of intensity and the situation is not life-threatening, you are likely experiencing some sort of a flashback.

The more you know about how trauma affects the human brain and nervous system, the easier it is to have a compassionate assumption. Often, it is easy for us to judge other people. We think they "should" or "shouldn't" act in certain ways. And typically, the yardstick we use for that judgment is whether or not we would have the same reaction. However, we have all had different experiences in life, so why would we all react the same way?

I have found that when I really understand what someone has been through, I also understand their behavior, and the beauty of EMDR therapy is helping people come to similar understandings in themselves. Because I have seen the root of people's pain so many times, it is easy for me to have a compassionate assumption. Whether it is problematic anger, addictions, depression, anxiety, or any other symptom, the presenting complaint is always something that helped the client to cope in the past.

The Answer and Compassionate Assumption

What do you notice when I say the following: "What if appreciating your problematic anger is the path to healing it? What if loving yourself instead of shaming and hating yourself can help you heal problematic anger?"

I don't miss the eyeroll that some people do when I mention self-compassion or self-love. Depending on your past experiences, these concepts can appear to be soft or even weak. But I would encourage you to sit with the idea rather than resisting it. As I previously mentioned, I only suggest it because I have found the compassionate assumption to be a necessary component in healing problematic anger as well as many other persistent habits and symptoms.

When you apply a compassionate assumption, you are *assuming* there is a reason to have *compassion*. With the SAFE EMDR concept of The Answer, we are always using a compassionate assumption. We are looking at the *adaptive value* of whatever is here—the benefit or value it gives you. For instance, when you experience a symptom, instead of thinking about how to make it go away, you'll be guided to go toward the symptom with curiosity and a basic, compassionate assumption that it has been helpful. This approach is very different from most other therapy approaches.

I was recently consulting with a mental health therapist who was stuck because her seven-year-old client—who had experienced a lot of major, overwhelming events in his short life—would take off running at school and at home when he felt frustrated. This was very concerning because of the danger of a seven-year-old running into the street or getting into other danger. I asked her to tell me what triggered the last example of running away. She reported that he was at school, waiting in line at the water fountain, but another student was apparently taking too long to use it. The child perceived this as a deliberate act to annoy him, though in all likelihood, the other student was trying to avoid going back to class.

The therapist said that she talked to her client about other options instead of running away. This problem-solving approach is common in psychotherapy but rarely effective, especially when clients have experienced trauma. Instead of problem solving, I recommended that she go toward the frustration to understand it further. These behaviors are like guards standing at the door of something more complex. The client's frustration and subsequent running away is a part of his Answer. In order to begin to explore this, we have to have an assumption that these behaviors have been helpful to him in some way. If we don't have this assumption, it is likely that we will problem solve and try to make his behavior go away before we truly understand how it has been helpful.

As you apply this to yourself, the concept of The Answer is the key to unlocking the door to an opportunity for healing. If we try to make the guards at the door (the feelings and behaviors that are driven by trauma) go away instead of befriending them, we will just piss them off, and they fight back instead of cooperating and opening the door. This practice of making friends with the guards at the door is a very small step but a powerful one. It is only possible to do this if you believe your symptoms are a result of the past and were once helpful. *That* is the compassionate assumption.

Anger and Compassionate Assumption

A compassionate assumption helps us get out of judgment and not take things personally, giving us the opportunity to see beyond our past and our anger responses. When we are utilizing a compassionate assumption, we assume that there is a reason for whatever is happening with another person—and that reason is not necessarily us. Not taking things personally helps us be calmer and more compassionate toward others.

The principle of a compassionate assumption helps us be curious instead of judgmental, which is a theme throughout the principles, concepts, and methods in this book. If you are in a state of curiosity, you cannot simultaneously be in judgment; it is impossible. If you are in a state of judgment and think you are being curious, you are likely being sarcastic instead of curious.

Of course, it's also true that most of our thoughts—including the judgmental ones—are automatic and habitual. It is a rare occasion that we sit down to think about something specific and our thoughts are intentional. Sensations, incoming data, opinions, beliefs, ideas, and certain painful memories are held together by raw emotion. Becoming aware that our experience of ourselves and others is mostly an illusion can be very helpful. Virtually anything we take "personally" is likely a misinterpretation. Even if someone is calling you a derogatory name, it is about them and not you. It only becomes about you if it somehow hits a hurt, unhealed past experience. To be clear, I am not condoning people calling you names or being rude, nor am I giving people a free pass to be jerks. But I am encouraging you to take a different, less personalized stance toward what you experience. Taking people personally and engaging with behavior that may not be rational doesn't do anyone any good.

This is especially true with experiences with strangers. The other day, I was leaving a parking lot and pulled into the middle turn lane of a busy street to merge in with traffic. A person pulled into the lane in front of me in an erratic manner, then put the car in reverse toward me and slammed it into park. A young woman got out of the car and began screaming at me. I had no idea what she was saying. I put my car in reverse and slowly backed up to get away from her. I immediately recognized the woman was not just reacting to me. It is highly likely that I did something to upset her, but no matter what I did, her reaction was not just about the incident. She had past, unresolved pieces of memory that were activated. I don't need to know what they were to know they were painful for her. Even her big reaction looked painful. It is easy to judge someone like her in that situation. However, judging her would have left me with residual anger, and holding anger toward a stranger would serve no purpose.

Coming to a compassionate assumption is not easy to do. It takes practice. However, changing your habit of uncompassionate, personalized assumptions can lead to a more peaceful life.

EXERCISE: Compassionate Assumption

Respond to the following prompts in a journal or using the worksheet available at http://www.newharbinger.com/54988.

1. Bring up a recent, mildly upsetting experience you had with a stranger and notice what you feel in your body.
2. What was your assumption about that experience?
3. Now imagine a scenario that would explain how that person's behavior is not about you. Make a list of situations that would help you to feel compassion toward that person.
4. If you have trouble making up a story that is helpful, imagine a painful childhood that person may have endured that may be influencing their behavior now.
5. Now bring up that recent experience again and notice if anything shifts for you.

If this exercise was difficult for you to do, it may be helpful to look for opportunities to practice applying a compassionate assumption. When you have an opportunity in public with a lot of people, find someone you feel judgment toward. Notice the story you make up about them. Then intentionally create a story about a difficult experience that person has recently endured. If necessary, use my son's idea, "She probably just lost her dog."

I have a philosophy about people that may sound radical; I believe if I really understand someone, I will love them. This way of viewing people helps me to keep a compassionate assumption and an attitude of curiosity toward people. It's likely that this is easier for me to do than someone who is not a psychotherapist. Being a SAFE EMDR clinician makes it even easier for me to have this view. As soon as I begin to work with a client, I am looking for ways their symptoms have been helpful to them. From the presenting issue a client brings to therapy through the entire SAFE EMDR therapy process, I am looking through a compassionate assumption lens as I apply the concept of The Answer to the client: as I look to how each symptom they report has developed to help the client maximize safety or connection. But if you intentionally begin to practice this view, it can become your new way of viewing the world—and yourself.

A Compassionate Assumption Toward Yourself

At first it may feel difficult to have a compassionate assumption about people who annoy you. I have found that it is even more difficult for people to apply the compassionate assumption to themselves. This is an important step for your own healing and will be very helpful through the EMDR process.

Shame and guilt are a common result of early, overwhelming experiences. When children experience trauma or neglect, they also often experience shame and guilt. It seems that it is normal for children to assume that the reason they are not being cared for is because something is wrong with them. As we look at this from the adult perspective, it is easy to see that this is not the case. But because of the nature of trauma, many of us are left with shame and guilt in our system from unprocessed past events.

Shame and guilt may have an adaptive value for human beings, but only if it serves to positively change your behavior. So if I do something and afterwards I experience a feeling of guilt or shame, I can use that to inform me and learn from that experience. If as a result of that I make a change, then those feelings are no longer useful. If they still stick with me even after I've changed—or if I feel shame and guilt for circumstances that weren't my fault—these experiences are actually more likely harmful. So, it's worth processing any sense of shame or guilt you feel from past events. If you made a mistake in the past but you learned from it and changed, it is best for everyone that you let go of any lingering shame and guilt. A compassionate assumption toward yourself can help you release the past and the unhelpful emotions attached to it.

Often when it comes to past regrets, we worry that explanations of our behavior may in fact be excuses for it. The important distinction between making an excuse and a compassionate assumption is that while excuses promote the continuation of a behavior, having a compassionate assumption promotes change and healing. It's actually the opposite of making an excuse for a behavior. An excuse may sound like, "I got so upset because that person was rude to me," followed by a global statement about the reaction like, "Anyone would react the same to that person." Another common statement after an excuse is, "Wouldn't that be upsetting to you?" A compassionate assumption, on the other hand, would be recognizing that the behavior—you getting angry—is in the past, and while you regret it, you have the desire to grow and learn from it. It is about taking responsibility for what happened and recognizing that there is some hurt part of you wanting to be healed. Instead of looking for support for feeling angry, as you would with an excuse, you are turning your attention to look inward for unresolved experiences that are being activated.

As you begin the process of looking at early, disturbing experiences that are at the root of your problematic anger, it is normal for shame and guilt to come up along with the memory. As this happens, if you can understand that those feelings are likely emotional fragments of the past that have been stored within you, it can be easier to allow them to move through your system. Without this view, you might get stuck in these feelings of guilt and shame and it can stop the process of growth and change.

Applying a compassionate assumption toward yourself is a way of changing a well-worn pattern of judgment toward yourself. Again, you can think about blame, guilt, and shame as guards. They are guarding the door to your authentic self. At one time, you needed their protection, and it is important that you appreciate how they have helped. Thank them and let them move on.

A part of EMDR therapy treatment includes what we call "cognitive interweaves." A cognitive interweave is what the therapist offers to the client in the EMDR therapy session when a client becomes stuck in the process. If a client gets stuck in guilt and shame in my office as they process a memory related to their adult experience, I might say something like, "Have you learned from that experience?" If they are reprocessing a childhood memory, I might say, "I wonder if that is what happened at the time?"

Since this is a self-help book, you can practice using these statements toward yourself. If you are feeling guilty about something that you did as a child, a compassionate assumption toward yourself is recognizing that childhood behaviors are often driven by a need for safety and connection, and consider your behavior through that lens. Things that are considered problem behaviors in children are often ways that a child is trying to regulate their emotions or get the attention and connection of caregivers. Children do what works toward the goal of connection and protection. Sometimes it doesn't appear to make sense, but if we have a compassionate assumption, we are more likely to look for ways this is true instead of assuming the child is just "bad."

In the case of the seven-year-old from earlier, with a compassionate assumption, I was able to lead his therapist to understand that his behavior was a reaction and not a conscious decision. Early in his life, the little boy had experienced the loss of his mother due to incarceration. To a child, the loss of a parent is a threat to survival. This overwhelming event was too much for his young nervous system to process and he was left with fragments of that event stored physically in his brain. If you think about the conditions that triggered his survival response of flight, running away makes sense. He was thirsty and believed that someone was intentionally keeping him from water. Can you see how this would relate to his earlier experience of not being able to access his mother as a young child? A mother provides nurturing, protection, and milk for a baby, and he was unable to access this when he was younger. These types of connections can only be made if we are looking for a good reason for a behavior to occur. Otherwise we are left thinking that he is just "being bad," which is never helpful or true.

So as you begin the process of looking at early painful experiences from your childhood, it can be very helpful for you to apply this type of assumption toward yourself. This allows for the experience to move through to a resolution instead of your tightening around it.

EXERCISE: Working Toward Compassionate Assumptions

In the following exercise, I would like to invite you to begin to use the principle of a compassionate assumption toward yourself. Again, you might find it useful to ask the question, "How is that helpful?" It may sound something like this example:

> I got mad at my partner and called him a name.
>
> As I remember doing this, I feel pressure in my stomach and this thought: "Why do I always lose my cool?"
>
> *How is that helpful?*
>
> Asking why is really a way of saying I don't know why.

How is that helpful?

It's likely that not knowing why is my mind's way of protecting a hurt part of me.

How is that helpful?

I got good at protecting myself from being hurt when my family made fun of me as a child. They would call me names sometimes. Calling names was the only way I felt I could get back.

How is that helpful?

I was doing the best I could to get through a rough time.

Try this technique with a recent experience, using the following steps.

1. Bring up a mildly upsetting recent time when you experienced blame, shame, or guilt toward yourself.
2. Notice the negative automatic thoughts that come up with the memory.
3. Whatever comes up for you, ask yourself, "How was that helpful?"
4. Continue asking "How was that helpful?" until you've uncovered a compassionate assumption for your behavior.

Chapter 4

Exploring the Principle of Healthy Boundaries

Do you feel frustrated by other people's behavior? Do you feel taken advantage of or that people expect too much from you? Or perhaps you find that other people seem irritated with you, and you're unsure why. These situations can arise when either our boundaries are being crossed or we're unintentionally crossing the boundaries of others. This can lead to increased tension, conflict, and problematic anger.

In SAFE EMDR, the principle of healthy boundaries works together with nonviolence, mindful awareness, and compassionate assumption to set the stage for a successful EMDR process. As you prepare to look at the origin of your problematic anger, the SAFE principles help to give you the best opportunity for success. They'll support your healing and positive transformation.

Understanding Boundaries

What do you think of when you hear the word "boundaries"? Maybe you think of a fence around your yard or the lines on a basketball or tennis court. Your personal boundaries are similar to those types of boundaries—they define where you end and another person begins. This applies to how we allocate our responsibilities, emotional energy, and time to ourselves and others. Being aware of the small ways you disregard your own and others' boundaries is the first important step to creating healthy ones.

Feeling angry can be a signal that your boundaries have been violated. Have you ever experienced any of the following?

- Said yes when you wanted to say no?
- Felt like you needed an excuse to say no to a request?
- Felt stuck in a conversation with someone you were not interested in talking to?
- Felt like you had to help someone get out of a problem you didn't create?
- Felt uncomfortable asking someone to pay back money they owed you?
- Felt manipulated into paying for something?
- Felt obligated to rescue someone from their mistakes?
- Allowed someone to take advantage of you because you didn't say no?
- Taken on more work or responsibility because you thought no one else could do it as well as you?

If you recognize yourself in any of these, you may be allowing your boundaries to be violated by others. This can lead to a sense of being taken advantage of that can fuel problematic anger.

Here are some signs that you may be violating the boundaries of others:

- Expecting others to know how you are feeling or what you want
- Problem solving for people who have not asked for your help
- Rescuing someone from a problem you didn't create
- Making decisions for others when you haven't asked permission
- Telling someone how they should feel, think, or believe

- Assuming there is only one right way to do something and that way is yours

Again, these behaviors can either be the source of anger or fuel it.

Anger is a great way to set a boundary. It is here because there is some way it has worked for you previously. As I have said before, it is important to appreciate how anger has helped you in the past in order to begin to change it. Most of the time, anger works to keep people away or stop people from doing something that you don't want them to do. If you have problematic anger, it could be due to difficulty setting boundaries in healthier, more peaceful ways. It is also helpful to practice using a compassionate assumption. Keep in mind that your current patterns with boundaries were developed because they were helpful in the past. Keeping this in mind can be helpful because the hurt parts of you might fear that this will strip away a familiar, protective, and adaptive behavior.

As we look at how anger has been helpful, we are also looking at early experiences in which you did not feel safe. These experiences formed your patterns of relating, including your boundaries. For some people, this feels like "blaming" other people for your current problems. The opposite is actually true. As you are able to understand the origin of your problematic anger, you are also taking responsibility for it. We will explore this more deeply in chapter 7, Step Two: Embracing Radical Responsibility. You may notice that blame is actually not a part of any of the SAFE EMDR process. Blame isn't helpful. But understanding and appreciating the origin of problematic anger can be very helpful if you would like to transform the anger into peace. This also allows you to observe your current patterns of boundaries with less guilt, blame, or shame.

Boundaries Are Patterns

Have you ever played a drum? Imagine beating a drum with two drumsticks. One stick hits the drum, and then the other stick follows, in a pattern. Now, imagine taking away one of the drumsticks, so just the lone stick is striking the drum; it is a very different experience.

The same is true for relationships. All relationships are patterns, and those patterns rely on both parties continuing their part. When one person stops their half of the pattern—as you might do, if you begin to set boundaries you haven't set before—the pattern will change. The other person may see the pattern change and begin to bang their drum louder to try to get you to continue. But they'll likely need to adjust, as will you.

As you begin to look at your patterns and consider which ones might need to change, it can be helpful to look at something as simple as saying no. Have you ever agreed to something that you didn't want to? Maybe it was a neighbor asking you to watch their cat while they go on vacation or a salesman selling you a car or a set of knives. You could have been caught off guard and agreed before you had time to think about it, or felt pressured to say yes when you really wanted to say no. This suggests that a boundary violation may have occurred, and you inadvertently played a role in it.

Saying no is the most basic form of setting a boundary, but some people feel they're being mean and that they need a good excuse before they can set that boundary. This could lead to having your boundaries crossed. A pattern of not being able to say no without an excuse is likely something you learned early in your life. Maybe it wasn't safe to tell someone no.

Our behavior is shaped by what is rewarded or punished over time. Just ask the people who create slot machines at casinos; they intentionally set the conditions and patterns of reward to make it most likely that you'll continue to push the button and play. This relates to the SAFE concept of The Answer, as we have been conditioned by years of punishment and rewards—most often in our family of origin via an unconscious, unspoken learning process. The result is the formation of certain automatic thoughts, feelings, and beliefs that continue to play a role in our lives.

These thoughts, feelings, and beliefs guide your behavior. Until you intentionally become aware of them, you remain a prisoner to your past. Whatever situations we were in as children and however we were treated becomes our blueprint for our adult relationships. That blueprint, whatever it looks like for you now, is not right or wrong—it just is. With awareness and a little effort, we can begin to discern what we want to keep about that blueprint and what we want to change.

Our patterns of creating boundaries, and how firm or rigid those boundaries are, depend on our early attachment experiences. As we adapt to maximize safety and connection, our boundaries are a part of that adaptation. If you experienced people invading or not respecting your boundaries in childhood, you may have difficulty recognizing the spectrum of options for setting boundaries. You may not have developed the ability to recognize cues of boundary crossing early enough to avoid feeling violated. This may result in a pattern of not creating clear boundaries at the outset and then reacting with a big anger reaction to finally set a firm one. This pattern can also result in the inability to create boundaries proactively or to recognize the small signals that your boundaries are being crossed in time to avoid an angry blow up.

The opposite is also a problem. If in your childhood you had a caregiver that depended on you for emotional support at a young age, your boundaries can have a murky quality. Since children depend on adults to care for them and provide support, when the roles are switched, it can create a lack of safety for a child. In this type of situation, the child becomes really good at reading the emotional climate of the room and especially people close to them. In a sense, they learned how to stay safe by making sure the people around them were safe. This pattern can later appear as controlling behaviors or a need to please others.

Another attachment pattern that can hinder boundary setting is a complete lack of any structure or boundaries in childhood. Young children require boundaries to be safe and feel secure. If you grew up in an environment that lacked boundaries—left on your own with little adult direction—this can also create an imbalance. Without experience or practice at setting and experiencing boundaries, it can be difficult to recognize how to create healthy ones. With this pattern, you may find yourself violating the boundaries of others and later feeling surprised at their reaction to you. You may also have difficulty distinguishing between healthy boundaries and feeling controlled.

If you recognize one of these patterns in yourself, it is important to acknowledge how you adapted to maximize connection and safety. That adaptation was necessary and helpful. None of our patterns are better or worse than others, they just are. Awareness of the pattern is the first step toward creating the boundaries that are most helpful for us now.

We all live with illusions from our past, ghostly remnants rooted in our childhood when we had little control over our circumstances. They are unwritten, unspoken rules that we continue to follow long after the rule maker is no longer with us, informing our behavior and agreements in our relationships. If we knew we had the choice, most of us would prefer to shed these limiting, unhelpful beliefs. What if you do have a choice, but you just don't know it yet?

Healthy Boundaries Create Safety

Clear, healthy boundaries create safety. These can be literal, physical, material boundaries, or boundaries that cannot be seen with the eye. Like a fence that keeps livestock safe from roaming off or getting injured, our boundaries also keep us safe. This safety can be both physical and emotional.

Physical boundaries help us define our space. Where you live is a physical boundary space. We create this physical safety with the literal boundaries of the walls of our home and locks on the doors. When we go into our space and lock the door, we feel safer.

Maybe you live in a space you share with others, where your personal, physical space is limited to a sleeping area or desk. Or maybe you live in a home with other occupants, where you share all of the spaces in your home with others. Or you may live alone in a home where your personal space encompasses everything within its walls. Whether it is a small bed or a large home that you call your own, the boundaries of this space help create a sense of safety and predictability.

Clear physical boundaries also help us avoid conflict. Think about state lines, the boundary of a property, or even a drawer that you keep personal items in. If the boundary has been clearly communicated with other people, there is less of a chance for conflict to occur.

Finally, clear, healthy boundaries help us create a sense of emotional safety. Sometimes we refer to this as trust. For example, when I am starting a meeting or training, I always strive to start on time. This is because I want to respect the boundaries of the people who took the time to show up and be on time. I also want to give a message to the people who were late that they can trust that I will be there and start the meeting on time. This is a boundary that helps to create emotional trust and a sense of emotional safety.

Awareness of Boundaries

A big reason the SAFE principles are so powerful is because they offer you awareness. Awareness of what you are currently doing is the first step toward change. To achieve awareness, you need to turn the lens of your view away from what other people are doing and toward yourself. The reason it is important for you to begin to look at yourself is that it is the only place you have real control. You can't force others to behave how you want them to. But you do have the power to change yourself and the ways you think about and respond to others and the world around you.

To reiterate, healthy boundaries are only about your behavior, not a way to control other people. They are not threats, power plays, or limits we can't or won't actually enforce. Boundaries allow others to have free will, which is crucial. (Of course, this isn't to say you should simply tolerate it if someone is doing something to harm you.) Boundaries offer choices and consequences that you can enforce. It is important that boundaries are stated clearly and that you are speaking the truth.

A Case Example: Creating Boundaries You Can Hold

A woman was feeling unhappy with her relationship with her partner. He would often go out drinking after work and not let her know he was going to be late, often staying out until after dark. She would pick their children up from school, go home, and start dinner. They would often have fights where she would demand that he stop drinking and going out after work. At times she would threaten to leave him, but the thought of raising children alone was overwhelming.

Threatening someone or yelling at them to stop their behavior may seem like setting a boundary, but it isn't. A true boundary can only be set when you have the power to enforce it. And this woman can't control her partner's behavior, which makes her demands that he stop ineffective. So what would an alternative to yelling and empty threats look like, to allow her to set a boundary that she can actually enforce? She might focus on actions she can feasibly take.

- *The next time you come home later than we've agreed upon, I will throw out your dinner rather than keeping it warm.*
- *If you continue to behave this way, I will find ways to separate myself from you in our home in order to live a peaceful life, until I can figure out a way to raise the children on my own (or perhaps with a relative who might take us in).*

Or anything else that she is ready to follow through with when it happens again.

What are some of the boundaries you might like to set with others in your life? You might have some immediate ones come to mind. Or maybe you'll need some time to figure out your answer to this question. Either way, give the following practice a try.

EXERCISE: Setting Small Boundaries

Changing any pattern requires practice. Becoming aware of your current boundary patterns and beginning to create new ones takes time. Be patient with yourself and try to notice how it feels to set small boundaries first before trying to tackle your most explosive relationships. Begin with something small, like saying no to a salesman without any explanation, or turning down an invitation to something you don't want to do by simply saying "No, I can't make it." Then notice how it feels to speak the truth and not explain yourself.

From Automatic Behavior to Choice

Again, what we learned growing up becomes our automatic way of being. But if you are an adult, you have choices. Moving from those automatic, unconscious patterns to seeing that you have choices is a big step on the path of change.

Of course, you also have to live with the result of your choices. But that, too, is a choice. If you hear yourself using the words "I have to" or "I should," that can be a signal that the past external rules are at play in your life. A simple change that can help with problematic anger is to change these statements to "I choose to…". How does this small change help?

When you are saying "I have to" or "I should," the control is outside of you. This indicates you have a belief that other people can make decisions for you. This belief was likely created by past experiences in which you felt forced to do things you didn't want to do and were punished if you didn't obey. You've likely repeated the pattern long after the punishment is over and there is no longer anyone forcing you to do anything.

If this is true for you, there is a way to break this cycle. That way is to practice a new pattern of recognizing choices.

Moving Away from "Shoulds" Experiment

Think of something that you believe you have to do and speak it out loud.

"I have to ________________." (Example: "I have to make dinner.")

Notice any tension or tightness in your body.

Make a list of other options. (Example: "I can order pizza." "I can ask someone else to make dinner." "I can fast until breakfast.")

Make a conscious choice. "I choose to ______________." (Example: "I choose to make dinner." "I choose to order out." "I choose to ask someone else to make dinner.")

Notice what changes in your body.

When you are thinking something or saying something, there is a part of your brain that hears what you say and takes it literally. When you make the small change from "I have to" or "I should" to "I choose," you have disrupted a pattern, and that literal part of your brain listens. Would you rather choose to do something or be forced to do something? Most of us would rather choose.

Recognizing that you have choices and actively making them will be taking a small step toward healthy boundaries. Clear, healthy boundaries also allow for choices to occur. Knowing what you have control over and what others have control over is a part of clear boundaries.

It is like setting up the overall structure of your relationships. If you make boundaries clear in the beginning, your relationships will all be more peaceful. Once the structure is in place, both parties have a better idea of what the rules are of the relationship.

When I am counseling couples in therapy, I am looking for the unspoken agreements in the relationship. Most of the time, those unspoken agreements are a result of a lack of clear communication at the start of the relationship. These agreements are really about boundaries.

One example of a common unspoken agreement is about responsibility for emotional responses. Partners will often blame the other person for causing their emotional reaction. The flip side of believing someone can make you angry is believing that someone can make you happy. Neither is true. This is a common belief, and a difficult one to grasp at first. But if you think about it logically, our emotional responses are much more complicated than that. What makes one person angry, for instance, might not affect a different person at all. The same goes for feeling happy. Just the recognition that your anger isn't caused by someone else is a major step in the right direction. It takes a lot of work to change this habit pattern, but the beginning of any change is increased awareness.

Boundaries, Anger, and Children

If you get angry with your kids, it may appear to be working. You are inducing fear in your child, and fear may stop behavior—but there is a cost. The cost is your relationship with your child and your child's self-esteem. In any relationship where fear is the management style, the backlash will likely be hidden. If you use fear to control your children, they will eventually lose respect for you and do things they want to do when you aren't looking. They may live in fear of you, rather than trusting you. There is also a good chance that they will not want to spend time with you when they are old enough to choose.

Yet another problem with using anger is that it is reactive. You have to see the behavior you do not want first in order to react with punishment. Then the child needs to remember what to do or not do later.

So what is the alternative? The best option is to set up a structure between yourself and your child that supports the desired behavior. This takes effort, creativity, and often collaboration to be effective. Children crave boundaries, and structure helps them feel more secure. You'll also need to ensure that you're well-regulated and resourced so that you don't blow up when your children push against the structures you've set—as children often do—or if the structure breaks down, which can happen in life.

Once you have set up the structure and begin sticking to it, with patience and persistence, you'll find you no longer have to use anger or threats to manage your child's behavior. And once the structure is set in place, it runs on its own. Then they are free to make choices within that structure.

When my three sons were in grade school, I started working full time. I was frustrated because the house was a mess and I always had to ask them to help me. I asked them to help me figure out a way for things to get done around the house. Together, we came up with a plan. We made a list of everything that needed to be done, then collaboratively divided the rooms of the house into three zones. We also divided up the duties in each zone. The kitchen duties, for instance, were divided into three: set the table, clean up the table, and load the dishwasher. The boys also ranked the three duties easy, medium, or hard. Each week they switched. Whoever had duties in the hard zone that week got special privileges, like choosing which seat they got in the car or where we went out for dinner. This zone system eliminated many arguments and the boys would manage it on their own. They would say, "Who has the hard job?"

By collaborating with them, they were invested in the program. This eliminated me constantly asking them to do their chores. Instead of "helping me," they had ownership of certain tasks. They would even remind each other to do their job, so I was completely out of the equation. A note about this method: One thing I did need to do was adjust my expectations for the quality of the way things were done. We can't really expect children to do many tasks as well as an adult. It is a gradual process to learn anything. So when this first started, I had to lower my expectations and allow things to be imperfect while appreciating the effort my children were making to help around the house.

By getting ahead of the game and creating structure, we are creating expectations. If you do this collaboratively with children, or any other people whom you're asking to do something, they are much more likely to buy into the process. No one likes to be told what to do and no one likes to be yelled at.

Boundaries, Anger, and Trauma

As I've explained earlier, trauma is when an overwhelming event occurs and our survival defenses take over. If you have problematic anger, it is likely that you have experienced some overwhelming events that would be considered trauma. Trauma affects our patterns of boundaries. If you experienced physical violence as a part of your childhood, you may have learned that conflict is dangerous. And even though the violence is no longer happening, it can be difficult for you to set healthy boundaries in a timely manner. Instead, you may only be able to set a boundary when you have been triggered into overwhelm and it comes out as an angry outburst.

In chapter 2, I introduced you to Anna, a woman who experienced extreme physical and sexual abuse by both parents. Prior to beginning the EMDR eye movement phase, we did some preparation that included exploring boundaries. One crucial boundary in the EMDR process involves the client's ability to tell the therapist to stop the eye movements, via an agreed-upon "stop signal" chosen by the client. Two options for the stop signal are raising one hand with the palm facing outward or making a "time-out" gesture with both hands.

When Anna tried the stop signal, she became upset. Just putting her hand up between me and her to tell me to stop felt dangerous to her. She reported feeling very anxious at the thought of doing it. So instead, we explored some other ways for her to indicate she would like to stop the eye movement.

As we began to process the early, traumatic memories, Anna got to a very difficult place and requested to stop the eye movements, so we did. "I wonder," I said, "what it feels like for you to ask me to stop and I stop?" She said: "Oh my God, that is exactly what I always needed." In that way, it became clear to us both that Anna asking to stop was a sign of real progress: she was setting a boundary, and seeing it respected. This experience helped her bring awareness to her new ability to set a boundary.

EXERCISE: Noticing Where You Might Need Boundary Work

To practice noticing the feeling of having your boundaries crossed, find a rope, tie, or scarf and some items that represent people with whom you have experienced boundary issues. Some items might be small toy figures, stuffed animals, small statues, or even a coffee cup can work.

1. Sit in a chair and put the scarf in a semicircle in front of you. Try to notice what feels just the right distance for you to create your personal space. You can experiment with different distances and configurations of the scarf.
2. Assign a person to the items you have selected. For example, the Power Ranger figurine may represent your boss at work.
3. Put the representation of your boss outside of the boundary you created and notice anything you are experiencing.
4. When you are ready, move the boss inside of your boundary and notice what changes.
5. Finally, adding whatever words you would like, remove your boss from inside your boundary and notice what changes.

Practicing setting boundaries when you are not in a stressful situation will make it easier to set boundaries with others when you feel the need to do so.

Chapter 5

Discovering Your Answer

What if the thing you do best is also the very thing that keeps you from being happy and free? What if your greatest strength is also the largest barrier to transforming anger into peace?

In this chapter, you will be invited to begin to explore your automatic ways of being in the world. You will also be invited to appreciate how these patterns and behaviors were developed as an adaptation to help you maximize safety and attachment when you were a child.

As I've discussed, the SAFE EMDR concept of The Answer is a simplified, practical way to look at the layers of the human experience. The Answer concept is a nonviolent, compassionate view of our current patterns and habits. It is a way to look at attachment patterns and patterns we created to survive and maximize safety. Sometimes I hear clinicians referring to The Answer as a "defense." They aren't completely wrong, but they are also not correct. It may be that many aspects of our Answer are here because they are protecting us, but that is only part of the picture. Our Answers are the automatic, habitual ways we respond to stress, loss, pressure, pain, desire, failure, success, boredom, writing a book, or building a house. There is an ancient quote, "How you do anything is how you do everything." This is a good description of the concept of The Answer. We learn to do things because at one point, they worked to maximize safety and connection, reinforcing the behavior. As we keep doing those things, we become really good at doing them.

Your Answer is the thing you do best—your greatest strength, your best skill—and the greatest block to happiness, intimacy, and healing. Whatever you complain about most is your Answer. If you go to a therapist, the thing you want to change the most is your Answer.

Over- and Underdeveloped Skills and Resources

We talk about The Answer in terms of strengths and resources because it is true; whatever way you adapted was helpful and worked to maximize your connection with your family and keep you safe. When I use the term "resources," I am referring to a behavior or reaction that helps or is useful in life. I use the word "overdeveloped" because that adaptation was frequently used due to its success. As a result, something else was "underdeveloped," or not useful in your family of origin. The reason I speak in terms of overdevelopment and underdevelopment instead of strengths and weaknesses is because the words "strength" and "weakness" have a judgmental connotation and do not fit with the SAFE principle of nonviolence. The practical reason for using these terms is that we want to sincerely appreciate the adaptive, helpful value of the way we changed our behavior or survived a difficult childhood.

Here are some examples:

- If your family valued following the rules, you may be overdeveloped at figuring out what the rules are and following them, but underdeveloped at being creative or spontaneous.
- If your family valued being logical, you may be overdeveloped at thinking things through and finding logical solutions, but struggle with recognizing or understanding the emotional aspects of situations, for yourself and others.
- If niceness was paramount, you may be overdeveloped at being courteous and noticing what others want, but underdeveloped at expressing your needs or handling and resolving potential conflict.
- If you experienced family violence, even if it was just yelling, you may be overdeveloped at emotional and possibly even physical detachment, but you may be

underdeveloped at staying present and calm in the face of another person's distress.

- If you experienced childhood loss or the illness of a family member who required extra care, you may be overdeveloped in self-reliance and underdeveloped at asking for or accepting help.
- If you grew up with an emotionally unstable family member, you may be overdeveloped at noticing others' emotions or energy and underdeveloped at setting boundaries and allowing others to be in distress without trying to fix it. Alternatively, this could also result in you being overdeveloped at ignoring other people's emotions and underdeveloped at connecting healthily with people who are hurting.
- If you experienced a lot of bullying or teasing as a child, you may be overdeveloped at putting up emotional defenses and underdeveloped in your ability to trust and have intimacy with others.
- If you grew up living in multiple homes with varying expectations, you may be overdeveloped at adjusting to the external world and underdeveloped at self-awareness or defining your own needs.

Since the concept of The Answer is the result of adaptations to maximize safety and connection to caregivers, it is a reflection of your attachment patterns and your survival defenses combined with your genetic tendencies. Simply put, your Answer was created and formed by three factors:

1. Your family culture or "bootcamp"
2. Trauma experiences
3. Genetics

You repeat behaviors that maximized connection with your family and kept you safe because they worked most of the time. The more you do something, the easier it is to do it again. These things become our automatic habits, patterns that we do without thinking about it.

Your Bootcamp

I may use the word "family" when describing your bootcamp, but what I am referring to here is the atmosphere and rules of your caregiving situation as a child. For some people, the bootcamp changed often due to lack of stable, consistent caregivers, as with those who grew up in multiple foster homes or moved between several homes with various caregivers. So whatever situation you grew up in is your bootcamp; you had to learn how to survive and adapt. Even if you rebelled against your family bootcamp, trying to be the opposite of them, your Answer was still formed by the adaptation to the experience.

Imagine a child trying to get approval from a parent or caregiver. What might the child do to achieve that goal? A lot will depend on the caregiver and their situation and preferences. In many cases, the caregiver is also at times a source of danger. This list of possible adaptations is not exhaustive but offers examples of what the "bootcamp" may be reinforcing.

- Being quiet and unseen
- Not noticing things
- Staying under the radar
- Staying busy
- Being funny or entertaining
- Ability to adapt to change
- Being helpful and noticing what others need
- Being good at sports
- Being good at academics
- Being strong

- Predicting what others want
- Reading the emotional climate
- Being independent
- Being sensitive
- Working hard
- Following rules
- Fitting in
- Looking good
- Being intelligent
- Standing up for yourself or others
- Being submissive
- Being nice
- Pulling your energy in and disappearing
- Being logical
- Being tough
- Being frugal
- Being generous
- Calming yourself alone
- Reaching out for help
- Saying what you want
- Repressing thoughts and feelings
- Keeping secrets
- Smiling through pain
- Getting others to help you without asking directly
- Lying or avoiding telling the truth

- Not seeing what is happening around you
- Being vigilant and observing everything around you

This list is just an example, as there are many other aspects that make up a family bootcamp or culture, messages that may be either explicit or unsaid. It is often the case that siblings have very different Answers in an attempt to find their unique place in the family. Siblings are also a factor in reinforcing or extinguishing certain patterns of behavior. In other words, if something works, we keep doing it. If something doesn't work, we tend to stop doing it.

Curiosity Experiment

I'd like to invite you to make a list of things that you see as a part of your bootcamp.

What were the expectations?

What was valued?

What did you get really good at doing?

What was not allowed or encouraged?

In what ways have you tried to be the opposite of your childhood bootcamp?

Use your journal to explore these questions.

Your Answer and DNA

In addition to the influence that our caregivers and families have on us through the environment we grew up in, we are also affected genetically by our DNA that is passed down, including what is called epigenetics. In the book *It Didn't Start with You*, author and lecturer

Mark Wolynn describes inherited family patterns that are passed down from generation to generation, often without awareness of their origins. We all have a tendency toward certain behaviors and patterns. Anger may have been handed down to you as a result of trauma that occurred generations ago in your family tree. Not only anger, but also illness, unexplained fears, limiting beliefs, and more. For the purpose of this book, it is not as important to know where the pattern or behavior came from as it is to accept that it does have an origin, which may be hidden from us. The reason this is important is, knowing that there is an origin, whether we know the culprit or not, helps us offer ourselves compassion. This also helps us explain the unexplainable, as some people tend to blame themselves for their symptoms despite having a great family and childhood.

This also applies to experiences your caregivers had that had an impact on their ability to freely give and receive love. Maybe you had a parent who lost their own parent early on or experienced a miscarriage prior to your birth. Those attachment losses will alter the patterns in your family. Your parents may be hesitant to connect with you for fear of experiencing another devastating loss, or they may overconnect and overprotect because of that same fear. As children, everything is about us, and we have no ability to see that the adults in our lives may be struggling with their own unresolved issues, so we are left feeling that we're to blame.

EXERCISE: Generational Stories

First make a list of unexplained behaviors, fears, or patterns that you find yourself experiencing. For example, fear of water, fear of being put in jail, or any other fear you may have that does not appear to have an origin. Or it may be a pattern like trust issues, attraction to unhealthy relationships, or other seemingly inexplicable patterns. Then make up a story about what might have happened in previous generations that may have been passed down to you. Feel free to be as creative as you want to be in this exercise. For a worksheet version of this exercise, see the online tools at http://www.newharbinger.com/54988.

Your Answer and Traumatic Experiences

When you have too many overwhelming experiences in your life, your body begins to see safe things as threatening.

How many times have you gotten angry with someone close to you because of the way they said something to you? How many times have people told you that you misunderstood what they said? This could be a result of past traumatic experiences, physically stored in your nervous system. You are seeing the world through those past events.

We have built-in protections to help us survive, and when our survival defenses are activated many times, they are more easily activated in situations that are not actually life threatening. Our physiological, automatic response to the threat of death or trauma is built in and adaptive. Even perceived threat will trigger our autonomic nervous system into one of our survival defenses.

Snake or a Stick?

I was hiking in the woods near my home and saw something out of the corner of my eye that appeared to be a snake. My system automatically reacted by jumping and yelling. With a closer look, I could see it was a stick and not a snake. I wasn't actually in danger, but there was a perception of threat and danger, and my survival defenses kicked in.

Humans are built to survive and we have a natural, physiological system that is geared toward helping us do just that. A survival response is not logical or thought out; it is an automatic, physiological response. Survival trumps everything else when it comes to our responses. Even if we had no actual traumatic experiences happen to us, or if we had lots of perceived trauma in which our survival defenses jumped in to help, we have created a pattern.

We now know that traumatic experiences in our lives are processed in a different way in our brain. In order to survive, certain parts of our brain shut down while other parts light up. One part of our brain that shuts down when we perceive danger is also responsible for processing the memory to make it feel like it is in the past. Since that area shuts down, that experience becomes stored in a fragmented, raw form in our brainstem. This leaves us vulnerable to overreacting in present situations due to reactivation of past traumas.

The World Looks Dangerous

Problematic anger is likely a result of not feeling safe. When you do not feel safe, anger is very helpful to bring action into your system to help you survive. However, if anger is a habit and has become a problem, it is likely your system is easily triggered into a fight response. The more you go into that fight response, the easier it is to go into next time. You begin to see the world through the eyes of trauma and it looks like a dangerous place, even when it is not. In essence, your system becomes addicted to and practiced at going into a defensive state of fight or flight. If you have experienced traumatic events or you have had many experiences of feeling overwhelmed, your system will be geared toward going into survival defenses.

In Stephen Porges's book *The Polyvagal Theory: Neurophysiological Foundations of Emotions, Attachment, Communication, and Self-Regulation*, he explains the connection between attachment and safety and how coregulation is an important part of the development of our nervous system. It is only when our nervous system is feeling safe that we are open to sensing the cues of safety and connection. This is called the social engagement system.

The state of your nervous system also affects your perception of yourself and the world around you. If your nervous system is in a state of fear, you will see the world as a dangerous place. In the service of survival, if your physiology is in a state of fear, you are not able to see the environmental cues of safety. And when you are in that physiological state, your perception of reality feels true even if it isn't. In other words, you don't know you are safe when you actually are safe.

Another important aspect of this theory is, the more you go into one of those states of activation, the better you get at going into that state. If you are in a state of safety a lot and able to be socially engaged and connected to others, it will be easy for you to feel safe and connected. You will be good at noticing cues of safety in an environment and you will only sense danger when it's actually present. If you go into fight-or-flight frequently, it will be easy for you to mobilize that state of getting angry and irritated, and you will see lots of reasons for feeling that way in the world. Your physiological state is telling your brain and body that the world is a dangerous place and it is important to protect yourself.

Another response to danger is to collapse and shut down. When you go into this state, you may feel depressed, hopeless, and have a hard time taking any action. Once your system goes into this place of shutting down, it requires time and patience to come out of it. In this state, your view of yourself and the world is numb and you may feel like there is no hope for change.

Our human autonomic nervous system is an amazing thing. We are born with the ability to survive horrific things. If you are walking in the woods and happily taking in the sights and sounds of nature, you are likely in a state of safety, ventral vagal activation. As you walk, a sudden sound like a grunt may send you into a state of sympathetic arousal; your heart rate goes up as your muscles tense and prepare to run. If you discover that it was just a tree blowing in the wind, you'll likely take a deep breath, maybe even laugh, and your body will go back to feeling safe in a few minutes. However, if you turn and see a mama bear with her cubs, that sympathetic arousal will automatically help do what you can to survive, either by running or fighting. If neither fight nor flight works, then you will enter the dorsal vagal state, appear dead, and go numb. Now the bear may no longer see you as a threat and will likely walk away. If not, the other, less desirable good news is you will not feel the pain of the bear eating you. As disturbing as that thought may be, it is kind of amazing that our human system has the ability to numb the pain of bad situations.

The bear scenario is an extreme example of how our nervous system kicks in to help us survive. The smaller ways that our system goes into these states are important too. It is very helpful to recognize what is happening in our nervous system so we can begin to recognize that our perception may be a physiological illusion. We may believe that something is threatening when it actually is not.

Having awareness of how your past experiences show up today is an important part of the path toward healing. You can begin to recognize the signs of the past clouding your present perception. Sometimes these physiological states even overlap. For instance, someone might say something to you that triggers a strong reaction in your system. You can still hear them, respond, and stay present as you notice your racing heart or your face beginning to feel hot. These moments of autonomic state overlap are opportunities to intentionally change your physiological state by using specific tools.

Here are some small ways of noticing your autonomic nervous system state:

Signs of feeling safe

- Making eye contact
- Openheartedness
- A sense of safety
- Feeling calm and connected
- Curiosity and compassion

Signs of fight or flight

- Worry and concern
- Anxiety
- Irritation
- Anger
- Fear
- Frustration

Signs of shutting down

- Shame

- Shutting down
- Hopelessness
- Feeling trapped
- Trouble speaking
- Numbness
- You don't feel pain

As you look at these lists, which do you go to more often? Can you recognize small signs that indicate your physiological state? What does this have to do with problematic anger and the SAFE EMDR concept of The Answer? Recognizing the adaptive and patterned nature of your nervous system can help increase your ability to have compassion and awareness, which gives you more options and flexibility of responses.

Finding Your Answer: The Answer Questionnaire

I'd like to invite you to answer these questions without putting a lot of thought into your answers. Write your answers down. Alternatively, or in addition, you can have someone you are close to ask you these questions and you can ask them in return. For a worksheet version of this exercise, see the online tools at http://www.newharbinger.com/54988.

1. What are you most proud of?
2. What is difficult for you to do?
3. What do you do under stress?
4. How do you handle extreme pressure?
5. How are you with deadlines?
6. How do you get your way?
7. Is it easy for you to say no?
8. Do you cry easily?

9. What do you do when you are upset?
10. Do you cry in front of others?
11. Would you call yourself a rule follower?
12. How do you deal with conflict?
13. In an emergency situation, what are you likely to do?
14. Is it easy for you to ask for help?
15. Is it difficult for you to accept help?
16. How convincing are you?
17. What are you likely to do when someone tells you no?
18. How do you handle negative feedback or criticism?

As you look at your answers to these questions, what patterns are you noticing?

- How do you regulate your affect, going from upset to calmer?
- Are you good at calming yourself, or better at reaching out to others for comfort?
- How are you with personal power?
- Are you good at making things happen, or better at going with the flow and letting others make decisions?
- How are you with boundaries?
- Are you good at being firm, or good at being flexible and accommodating?
- How are you with verbal expressions?
- Are you good at verbal communication or better at listening? Are you able to easily put words to your emotions?
- How good are you at influencing others?
- Are you good at convincing others or better at noticing what other people want?

What you have learned in this chapter will be used throughout the rest of the book. I've highlighted the role of unprocessed memories in fueling your reactions, and how you have naturally adapted to maximize attachment and safety based on your experiences in your family of origin. These behaviors and ways of being become the water you swim in and the way you react to the world.

As you move through the rest of the book, I would like to invite you to notice the ways these behaviors and patterns attempt to help you. If possible, acknowledge them and thank them for their efforts, and appreciate how they helped you when you needed them. Sincere appreciation paves the path for transforming anger into peace.

This understanding and appreciation of your adaptive patterns is a very important part of healing anger. As you experience the next SAFE EMDR steps, this view of yourself will be like novocaine at the dentist, helping reduce the pain of looking at your unhealed memories.

Part 2

Transforming Your Anger into Peace

Chapter 6

Step One: Making the Decision to Change

On a scale of 0 to 10, 0 being not at all and 10 being absolutely yes, how much do you want to change your problematic anger? Take a moment to write down a number. And on a scale of 0 to 10, 0 being not at all and 10 being absolutely yes, how uncomfortable are you willing to be in order to change your problematic anger?

Changing habits and patterns is difficult. Just like starting a new exercise regimen, real change often includes some discomfort or pain. That is why it is important to make adequate preparations prior to examining the root of problematic anger. It is also very helpful to make a conscious commitment to change.

When I agreed to write this book, I made a commitment. Once I committed to it, I couldn't just back out. I was completely dedicated to seeing it through to completion.

In this chapter, I will help you discover your true motivations for changing your problematic anger patterns. An important part of that process will be to help you find the problem that is only about you. Although other people can inspire and motivate you to want to change, the decision to change is most effective when you fully recognize how it is a problem for you. We will also look at some common unconscious patterns that may be fueling your anger.

How Is Anger a Problem?

How is anger a problem for you? I would like to invite you to write down your answer to that question. If we were together, I would keep asking you that question until you finally got to an answer that only had to do with you. It might go something like this.

Me: "How is anger a problem for you?"

You: "I get upset when people tell me what to do."

Me: "How is that a problem for you?"

You: "I don't like to be told what to do."

Me: "How is that a problem for you?"

You: "It makes me mad."

Me: "How is that a problem for you?"

You: "I react toward the person I see as trying to control me."

Me: "How is that a problem for you?"

You: "They react back to me and it creates a big blow up."

Me: "How is that a problem for you?"

You: "It can create tension and unhappiness for weeks."

Me: "How is that a problem for you?"

You: "I want to have a happy, peaceful relationship. And I don't want to get a divorce."

Clarifying your motivation to change is important, but understanding that you *want* to change is the most important thing of all. The reason for change has to be about you, and what you stand to gain or lose as a result. Keeping this motivation in mind is an important first step. Ultimately, the answer to "How is that a problem?" should end with something that is *only* about you. For most, the desire for change stems from a longing to no longer feel unhappy, disconnected, or unfulfilled, and to experience happiness, fulfillment, and freedom, or something similar. These are universal desires.

EXERCISE: How Is That a Problem?

I would like to invite you to do this exercise for yourself. Write down in your journal what you see as the current problem, then continuously ask yourself, "How is that a problem?" or "How does that limit me?" until you are very clear about what you ultimately want.

Drama Triangle

Problematic anger is often linked to unhealthy ways of managing conflict, typically learned from our family of origin. In order to get to a healthier conflict style, it is helpful to understand your current unhealthy style.

The Drama Triangle, created by Stephen Karpman, is an example of an unhealthy pattern that is often unconscious (Karpman 1968). In the Drama Triangle, there are three participants: the Victim, the Rescuer, and the Persecutor. When we apply the concept of The Answer to the Drama Triangle, we understand that we take on one or more of these roles because it was helpful to us in the past. As you read the descriptions of each type below, keep in mind that each of these styles typically develops out of an adaptation, not necessarily a conscious choice. All three participants in the Drama Triangle theory would likely prefer freedom to being stuck in this drama-filled pattern.

The Victim

The person who is often in the role of the Victim learned that it was dangerous to be responsible. A person who is unconsciously in this role has learned to be helpless, stuck, and dependent on someone else to solve their problems. They feel like other people or situations are creating their suffering and there is little or nothing they can do about it. This can foster feelings of shame and a sense of internal defectiveness, as well as hindering their ability to see opportunities and take personal control. Because the Victim believes the problem and the answer are outside of them, they can flip to being the Persecutor as they blame others for their pain and situation. They can also become angry because the Rescuer jumps in to help them without consent or permission.

The Victim seen through The Answer: The Victim has likely adapted to stay safe by not fighting back. It was likely dangerous for a person in a Victim role to show direct personal power by saying no or setting a boundary. They may have experienced frequent situations where their autonomy was undermined, or where they felt physically or emotionally unsafe, opting to submit in order to avoid more trauma. Trapped in a survival mode of submit and collapse, they experience feelings of hopelessness and worthlessness, further reinforcing their negative self-image. EMDR reprocessing of memory fragments of the past experiences can be very helpful to release the physiological remnants of fear in the brain. Individuals with this type of history and pattern can benefit from developing a stronger sense of personal power and agency. However, without awareness, they can become reliant on a need to be rescued, despite how this behavior continually undermines their personal power. The real need is for someone to provide encouragement and support as they develop their ability to set boundaries, say no, and ask for what they want and need.

The Rescuer

The person who is often in the role of the Rescuer is the typical enabler. They often have difficulty asking for help for themselves, but hyperfocus on the needs of others. They will often rush to protect, solving problems without asking permission. This is often fueled by their difficulty in tolerating others' pain. Believing others to be incapable of self-sufficiency, they compulsively step in to the rescue. They likely have trouble saying no or creating healthy boundaries, and often feel like people take advantage of them. They feel compelled to put their own wants and needs aside to come to the aid of others, often resulting in resentment. The Rescuer can flip to being the Persecutor and get angry because they feel others haven't reciprocated or appreciated what they have done for them.

The Rescuer seen through The Answer: The Rescuer learned to be hyperaware of what other people need and want. They likely had many experiences of overwhelm and a lack of safety, determining that the best way to maximize safety and connection was by managing the feelings and needs of other people. They likely felt they were on their own, with little or no protection from caregivers, and focusing on others may have provided some distance from this pain, which is often fueled by the belief that they aren't enough. By helping other people, they were able to connect, helping them feel safer. It was not useful or helpful for them to focus on their own needs or desires.

The Persecutor

The person who occupies the role of the Persecutor is angry, critical, controlling, and blaming. A person in a Persecutor role often feels attacked or provoked by others, sometimes resorting to verbal or physical violence. They have a very fragile sense of self and are easily offended, with very little tolerance for anyone with a different opinion or idea. They have difficulty trusting others, often seeing them as incompetent. Since both the Victim and the Rescuer at times take on the role of the Persecutor, the Persecutor reflects the worst of both other roles. The Persecutor believes the reason for their anger is what other people are doing, reflecting the Victim, or becomes angry and resentful because they believe no one appreciates them, reflecting the Rescuer.

The Persecutor seen through The Answer: If someone is stuck in the role of the Persecutor, they have learned that the only way to have personal power is to have power over others. They likely experienced severe and overwhelming traumatic experiences, possibly where being wrong was dangerous. Along with a fear of vulnerability, they are unable to look within to see the role they are likely playing in their own misery. Without taking personal responsibility, it is very difficult for someone really stuck in the Persecutor style to have real power to make a change in their lives.

We all fall into these categories at one time or another in our life. Maybe you see yourself in all three roles to some degree. As you become more aware of the unhealthy patterns you are currently stuck in, it is easier to become aware of other options. It is also important to remember that these patterns were formed because they were helpful at one time.

The good news is that there is a way out of this unhealthy, dramatic way of living. That way out includes the SAFE foundational principles we discussed in the earlier chapters, along with developing an appreciation for how these unconscious patterns developed to help us adapt.

The Drama Triangle is also referred to as the Trauma Triangle because it both stems from unresolved trauma and creates more trauma experiences for all involved. All three roles in the Drama Triangle come from seeing the world through the lens of unprocessed, overwhelming experiences. The Victim, Rescuer, and Persecutor all have difficulty taking personal responsibility and creating appropriate boundaries. When people experience a lot of overwhelming, traumatic events, they are often living in a constant state of feeling unsafe due to the remnants of the past left in their brain, which are constantly triggered and thus relived. If you experienced a lot of fearful events in the past, you will continue to see the world as a dangerous place until those past events are adequately processed. Those pieces of the past are the hidden fuel source that keeps anger and drama alive. In order to have the best chance of resolving the past, understanding your role is very helpful.

Although understanding your patterns can be helpful to make the decision to change, it may not be enough. The reason EMDR therapy is so popular is because we have realized that we cannot think our way out of trauma responses. Seeing the unhealthy patterns and increased awareness of how we play a part in those patterns is very helpful. But when the past fragments of our overwhelming experiences are ignited, our bodies and minds react as if the past is here now. Since those stored memories are fragmented, they can appear as a big emotion and a physical sensation of fear without the context of the past. So we believe that our reaction is really about right now. When that happens, it is very difficult to access the knowledge that our reaction is about us and not the other person.

A Case Example: Feeling Controlled

Jack came into therapy because his wife was threatening to divorce him. He reported that she was very controlling all the time, which was upsetting to him. I asked him to give an example of her controlling behavior. He said he was recently backing out of the driveway when she grew upset that he was going too fast and he'd forgotten to put his mirrors out. She stated she was afraid, but he insisted he had it under control. He was honest and said he'd yelled at her and told her to stop trying to control him. This small event spiraled into a day-long argument, which he reported had happened many times. In the end, his wife told him she wanted to live a peaceful life and was planning to leave him.

When I asked him what he would like to get from therapy, he stated that he knew she was overreacting and he wanted to learn to just ignore it and not get upset by it.

Because Jack saw his problem as outside of himself, I realized we had some work to do. This is often the case in therapy; someone comes in believing the reason they are reacting is because of someone else. Whether we are in therapy or not, the only person we have the ability to change is ourselves.

As we looked more deeply at Jack's problem, we discovered some patterns and past experiences that were likely keeping him stuck in a cycle of problematic anger:

- *Jack saw his wife's fear reaction as an attempt to control him. When she had this reaction, he felt like she was blaming and criticizing him. Because he had this view, he would become instantly angry and would yell at her.*

- *Jack stated his wife has a history of feeling unsafe in childhood and difficulty trusting. She had told him many times that when she is afraid and he yells at her, it is the opposite of what she needs at that moment, and that it would be helpful if he would recognize her fear and let her know he cares about her feelings. Jack stated he believes doing this would be admitting he is wrong and taking blame for something he didn't do.*

- *Looking at Jack's Answer, or adaptive strength, he reported being a hard worker. He is also really good at noticing the emotional climate of the room—especially when someone is upset—and tries very hard to avoid upsetting others. He tries hard to please his wife by doing things he thinks will make her happy, and often feels like she doesn't appreciate his efforts, jumping on him if he slips up like when he was backing out of the driveway. I recognized that avoiding being wrong or blamed may have been useful for Jack in the past but is now partially fueling the conflict.*

- *Looking more deeply into Jack's history, he had a very authoritarian, alcoholic father who was easily triggered into rage, resulting in multiple experiences of severe physical and emotional punishment from a very young age. He reported that his father would often force him to do manual labor to exhaustion, and was often critical about the way he completed the work, demanding perfection. He would often tell Jack he was stupid or incompetent for not doing things right. Jack reported these experiences left him with a feeling of being defective.*

- *When asked if he thought his past experiences and current reactions were contributing to the problems in his marriage, Jack reported that he didn't feel like the past was affecting him, but he would like to be able to ignore his wife's overreactions.*

In the above description, can you see any way that applying the concepts of SAFE EMDR could be helpful to Jack? Here are some questions to consider:

- How are Jack's past experiences influencing how he views his wife's fear reaction?
- How is it understandable that Jack would run into difficulty if he believes his behavior is contributing to his wife being upset? How could his wife's fear reaction feel dangerous to him?
- How did Jack's Answers and adaptive strengths that he developed work to maximize his safety and connection in childhood? How was that helpful?
- How might the conclusion of "being defective" play into the way Jack experiences his conflict with his wife?
- How is it understandable that Jack believes that the answer to his problem with his wife is outside of him? How is it reflective of his Answer that he doesn't believe his past has an impact and would like to focus on not reacting to his wife's unreasonable fear?

For my part, using the principle of compassionate assumption, I assume there is a good reason for Jack's view of the conflict with his wife. I notice that Jack experiences his wife's emotional reaction as an attempt to control him. As I notice that, I begin to wonder if Jack felt "controlled" in his childhood. I am also curious about how feeling blamed is upsetting for Jack. I'm wondering if being blamed in the past resulted in unpleasant consequences.

As I hear about Jack's Answer, I imagine how it was helpful to avoid conflict and become really good at noticing any sign of someone being upset or mad at him. It's clear he also learned how to work hard to try to please people and avoid being "in trouble." He was good at doing things he didn't want to do and ignoring what he wanted, along with seeing the problem as outside of himself and trying to manage what he views as "crazy" behavior.

As I heard Jack's history, I could completely understand how he developed these skills as a natural adaptation to maximize safety and connection in childhood. His Answers helped him to make the best of living with an unpredictable, violent, critical parent. They also became patterns that were the automatic ways he responded to stressful situations and to conflict. By appreciating the adaptive value of those things, it was easier for Jack and me to discuss how these behaviors were helpful in the past but potentially overused and less necessary in his relationship with his wife.

Although it took us some time to really recognize and appreciate how Jack developed these patterns, once he understood (and felt understood), he was more open to taking responsibility for his own behavior, and to examining how the past traumatic experiences with his father shaped the ways he behaved now. I was able to explain that, although those experiences were far in the past, it appeared that some remnants of them were still residing in his brain. He was able to understand and appreciate how participating in the EMDR process could help him be less reactive to his wife and possibly save his marriage.

EXERCISE: Updating Your Younger Self

Now, let's turn to your own case. At this point in your journey, have you made a decision to change how you behave, especially when it comes to expressing problematic anger? Or are you perhaps still focused on how others in your life are the problem? If you feel defensive about your situation, criticized, or controlled, can you make an effort to push past these feelings to what you know you're responsible for? One way to do this is to imagine the younger you who experienced similar things in the past. Imagine letting that younger part of you know that the past is over and you are safe now. Take some time to write about what this might look like for you.

Acknowledging Your Role in Change

Making a decision to change is helpful only if you really understand how you are playing a role in the issue you are facing. The SAFE EMDR principles and concepts help to make that process more likely to succeed. If what you want to change involves another person, it is very unlikely you will have success if your focus is only on that other person's behavior. And as with Jack, finding a way that the past is present can help you see how you are participating. To Jack, his initial goal of not reacting to his wife's behavior appeared to be about him, since he wanted to change his own reaction. However, the problem in his mind was still his wife and her behavior. He wanted to be able to tolerate behavior he saw as an overreaction; he was unable to see that he was overreacting to her behavior in turn. If it was truly just about his wife and her reaction, he would have had the space to hear her and be curious about what she needed at that moment. Instead he became instantly defensive and felt criticized and controlled. He was, in essence, experiencing a flashback from his unresolved trauma with his father, which played a part in the story he was telling himself about his wife.

As we walked through the SAFE EMDR process, he was able to see how his past traumatic events and the ways he adapted to them were contributing to the conflict with his wife. He was also open to looking at those past events that were still present and "hot" in his brain. Then he had a chance to reprocess those experiences with EMDR. Once he processed those events, he was able to finally stop reacting to the hidden fragments of the past. Then he could see that his wife's reactions were more about her than him, and once he wasn't taking it personally, he could be there as an emotional support for her, deepening their connection.

Chapter 7

Step Two: **Embracing Radical Responsibility**

Would you like to have more control over your emotional state? Would you like to have the power to choose the way you respond to the world? Would you like it if situations and people stopped having power over your internal state? In other words, would you like it if situations and people stopped pissing you off?

If you said yes to any of the above questions, I would like to invite you to intentionally open yourself to the possibilities of this chapter. You have the key to emotional freedom: a life without compulsive, problematic anger. Now you just need to find the door and choose to open it.

In the first sixteen to eighteen years of our lives, we develop patterns of how we view ourselves and the world. As children, we're also at the mercy of others and our circumstances. Even if you had parents or caregivers who encouraged you to make conscious choices, it is common to be stuck in the belief that we are controlled by outside forces and opinions. Unless we make a conscious effort to expand our awareness to other possibilities, we are stuck in that old paradigm of being the victim of the outside world.

I recently read that some chicken farmers use the "free range" label as a marketing ploy, but the chickens are really crowded in a pen. They can do this because they have added a small door to the pen that can be opened for the chickens to go into the pasture. But when chickens have been raised in a crowded pen, they do not see the option of going out into the pasture. Even when a door is opened, they remain in the crowded pen. They don't realize going out into the pasture is a possibility.

The experience of expansion is frightening for many people. Imagine a chicken who has been feather-to-feather with other chickens since birth accidentally walking outside into an open pasture. The chicken would likely feel vulnerable and afraid of this very different environment. Similarly, even if our current state of emotional bondage is uncomfortable, it is a known discomfort that we are accustomed to feeling. So in a strange way, it feels safe.

Letting go of ideas, behaviors, and views that limit us can make us feel vulnerable and insecure. However, until we are able to tolerate the discomfort of expansion, we will remain caged in our old patterns, just as the chickens remain stuck in their pens.

Many of the concepts in this book are a paradigm shift. A "paradigm" means the patterned way you see the world and yourself. Are you open to the possibility of expansion, to other options, if they help you experience freedom from problematic anger?

Understanding Radical Responsibility

Radical responsibility is a concept that can be difficult to understand. Let's talk about what it is *not* about. Radical responsibility is not about blaming others or yourself. It is not about letting people who have hurt you "off the hook." It is not about being responsible for anyone else, only yourself. It is also not about taking over the responsibilities of others through action. It is only about taking the fastest route to empowering yourself by taking responsibility for the only thing you have the ability to control—yourself.

People often come into therapy believing the problem is outside of them. This is common and understandable. Imagine how much work it would take to make change happen if we were only focused on changing other people. Even if the plan is to remove yourself from the people and situations that you believe are the problem, if you haven't looked at the part you were playing in the relationship or situation, you will likely find yourself in the same situation. Same situation, different person. Because you haven't expanded your awareness to include your part in the unwanted pattern, you will continue to create situations in which you find the same misery.

Have you ever met someone who has been through multiple relationships and possibly multiple marriages and divorces? When asked what happened, they may say something like, "I have a broken picker." They sincerely believe that the only problem is they continue to pick people who "aren't right" for them—that their partners are the problem. It is very unlikely a person who has that worldview will ever find true happiness, freedom, or intimacy. A person stuck in this pattern is attempting to find happiness through others—and thus also finds misery through others.

No one can make you happy, no one can make you miserable, and no one can make you angry. Can you imagine the possibility of this concept?

I'd like to invite you to read that sentence again and notice how you respond to that statement. Is there any part of you that doesn't believe it is true? Maybe you believe it is all untrue and you can give examples of how people have made you happy, miserable, or angry. What if I told you that the *illusion* of believing that someone outside of you can make you happy, miserable, or angry is the problem?

I was recently watching an interview of a professional golfer who had just won a major championship. The reporter asked him about his reputation for having very little emotional reaction on the golf course. The golfer said, "You won't see me fist pumping when I make a good shot or getting upset when I make a bad shot. Both of those are the same thing and they prevent me from focusing on the next hole." That golfer understands the power of having control over his emotional reactions.

I'm not saying you should not have emotions. Emotions are important and make life interesting and rich. What I am saying is, the ability to recognize that the source of your emotions is within you and not outside of you is a major step in experiencing emotional freedom.

In my office, I have faced this issue with clients many times. The belief that the world or other people can make us feel happy, unhappy, or angry is such a difficult one to change. One way I demonstrate this is by inviting the person to try to make me happy, miserable, or angry.

Or to imagine trying to make someone like the Dalai Lama angry. Once you really understand that we are all responsible for our reactions, you are empowered. You cannot be jerked around by people or life. Nor will you be the one to jerk others around. In order to achieve this, you need to change your focus from wishing the world would change to looking within yourself and being curious about your reaction.

Many people believe that the problems they have in life are externally caused and believe that if they could just have a better job, more money, a better partner, or other external things, they could finally be happy. While there are many external events that create problems, the fastest route to freedom is identifying and resolving the internal issues or patterns that leave you vulnerable to being triggered by the outside world. When you do this, you become the agent in charge of your own behavior. You're not subject to your anger.

What do you notice when you hear the word "responsibility"? What do you notice in your body? What thoughts come to mind? What memories do you have? For most people, the word "responsibility" is linked to blame or the burden of taking on something, or being forced to take action. When you look at the word "responsibility," it is actually the ability to respond. Responding is the opposite of reacting. When you can respond instead of react, you are in control of yourself and your emotional state.

Recognizing responsibility is also not about taking action. What I am referring to is noticing your response to situations. When something happens outside of you, what happens for you? Do you have a reactive, compulsive, knee-jerk reaction? Or do you know that you have options and decide how you respond to the outside world?

The Glasses of the Past

Our perception—the way we see the world and ourselves—is because of our past experiences. This is the way the human brain and memory work. Our memories of the past become a way to understand and make sense of our present experience. Think about seeing a car speeding down the street. If you never had the experience of seeing a car before, you would be amazed and maybe frightened to see a car speeding by you. But because you know what cars are, you're probably unfazed. In order to make sense of the world, our memory bank puts things in categories. The human brain is an amazing organ; it manages to be the most efficient by remembering patterns and storing our experiences—in fact, that's how learning happens. It is natural for our past to color the way we see the present. However, in terms of problematic anger, our past negative experiences may be creating a misperception of the present. Just being aware of this can be very helpful in the beginning of change.

Do you hold a grudge? When was the last time you felt angry, hurt, or took something someone said or did "personally"? Maybe you are hanging on to something someone said or did a year or more ago—maybe even decades ago. When you remember the thing someone said or did, you may even be able to conjure up images, sounds, intense emotional feelings, or other experiences that keep that painful experience alive in you. What if the reason that event was so painful and memorable is because you have an unhealed wound from the past that became activated by that experience? EMDR therapy is a way of finding those experiences and helping you to release the emotional charge they hold for you. When you can do that, the present experiences no longer have the "extra fuel" of the past, creating a more intense reaction for you. Even if you decide to never actually do EMDR therapy and you are just reading this book as a self-help guide, beginning to take personal responsibility for your reactions will be helpful. That personal responsibility begins when you become curious about a big emotional reaction you experienced and wonder if you have an earlier, unhealed wound that is adding "extra fuel" to the present experience.

Most of the time when we become offended or reactive to something someone says or does, we justify our reaction as "righteous" and we have a judgment that something outside of us has created the pain we are experiencing. As I say this, I want to be clear that I am not referring to global injustices in the world—abuse of power, racism, discrimination, war, and other very disturbing events that are happening. These things are wrong, and it is important that we do whatever we can to correct them in our world and help the people who are victims of them heal. What I am referring to here is judgment and offense as these manifest in our lives. We're guiding you to work with problematic anger, to heal it, by focusing on the fastest route for you to take. That route is inward.

Every time we have a big reaction that is fueled by past experiences, we are strengthening that response. This is another good reason for considering the path of radical responsibility. Like I have stated before, the human system is geared toward repeating patterns. That is why habits are so difficult to break. Every time we overreact, it is more likely we will overreact again. We have reinforced that pattern. Just by intentionally becoming curious about our reaction without changing anything else, we have started to change the pattern.

Another thing to be curious about is the circumstances of your relationships—including the unspoken agreements you might have with people in your life that fuel your problematic anger.

Unspoken Agreements

As you begin to look inward when you have a big anger reaction, you have started the process of looking at your part. In all relationships, we have agreements that keep the patterns of that relationship going. Rarely are those agreements spoken. Most of the time, the patterns of a relationship form organically because they work.

For example, I have a sister with whom I am very close. However, she will rarely reach out to me for connection. If I want to see her or talk to her, I am the one who reaches out. For many years this agreement was unspoken. I would often feel hurt and take it personally that she didn't reach out to me, yet I rarely said anything. There were times that I passive aggressively went for longer periods of time without reaching out, just to see if she noticed. As we got older and hopefully wiser, I finally spoke about the previously unspoken agreement. I said something like "I'm always the one who calls you. Why don't you ever call me?" She said, "I don't know, that's our agreement." She also explained that she is like that with everyone. She has a difficult time reaching out. Just speaking the agreement helped us to both laugh about it.

When I am counseling couples, their unspoken agreements are some of the first things I try to help them uncover. The reason this is important is because most people don't see it as an agreement—especially when it comes to things about the other person they may resent. But a relationship is based on patterns between two people. You may not like that you're agreeing to certain things, but the fact that you are continuing the pattern means you are agreeing to it.

Identifying the unspoken agreement gives you and the other person a chance to reevaluate the agreement. This is a healthy way to take personal responsibility for your part of any relational pattern in your life.

EXERCISE: Unspoken Agreements

Think of a relationship in which you feel there is an imbalance or something that you feel resentful about. Then answer the following questions in your journal. (For a worksheet version of this exercise, see the online tools at http://www.newharbinger.com/54988.)

Write about the imbalance or the pattern you feel resentful about.

Fill in the blanks of these sentences:

I don't like it that ________________.

I am agreeing to ________________.

The unspoken agreement I have made is ________________.

The new agreement I would like to make is ________________.

Take a moment to write about your part of this pattern. How does it reflect your Answer? How is it something that you seem to do a lot in relationships? How is it something you are good at doing?

If possible, write directly to the part of you who developed this pattern. Write about how that part of you has been helpful and give it appreciation.

Now tell your Answer about the new agreement you would like to make with the person you're in relationship with, and how that new agreement will be helpful.

Make a plan to talk to the person who is the other party of the unspoken agreement. If possible, take full responsibility for the pattern without trying to place blame on the other person. It is best to leave that—the matter of their responsibility and whether and how they'll take it—up to them.

Case Example: Isn't That Normal?

Brandon came into therapy at the request of his wife. He is a very involved and dedicated father. He enjoys his children, volunteers at their school, enjoys playing games and sports with them, and is very dedicated to being a good parent. I asked Brandon what he would like help with, and he stated that his wife believes that he overreacts and yells when he is worried about their children being hurt. Then he added, "I think it is normal to get upset if I think my kids are hurt."

I asked him to give an example of a recent time this happened. Brandon reported that his son had a recent medical emergency due to a severe allergic reaction to nuts. Afterward, Brandon was on high alert when his son was eating. On one occasion, his son was eating something and Brandon asked him what it was. When his son didn't immediately answer, Brandon panicked and yelled, "What are you eating!" Brandon said to me, "Wouldn't any parent get upset if they were afraid their child may be hurt?"

I could see that Brandon had a hard time seeing that he had other options. I was very curious about how this pattern developed for him. When someone uses this global response—"Wouldn't anyone…?"—I begin to wonder how it has been adaptive for them to focus on the outside world instead of their own reactions.

I asked Brandon to tell me more about himself and his life as a child. Brandon was the oldest of five children. From a young age, he was expected to be responsible for helping his siblings. When Brandon was twelve years old, his parents divorced. Brandon and his siblings lived with his mother and rarely saw their father after the divorce. Brandon's mother had to work extra hours to support their family, leaving Brandon in charge of watching his younger siblings. A twelve-year-old is not really capable of taking on the responsibilities of parenting, but this was the situation Brandon was forced to be in.

When a child is in a situation where they are given more responsibility than what's appropriate for their age, it is common for them to use anger to cope. A twelve-year-old put in charge of four younger siblings for extended periods of time is a big job. Since he was their sibling and not a parent, he didn't have the skills or the authority to manage his siblings. Knowing his mother was already overwhelmed, he worried about getting in trouble if his siblings misbehaved, and often panicked when he was in charge and couldn't get everyone to cooperate. Because he often felt frustrated and ineffective while managing his siblings, he often became angry—and when he was angry or threatening to his siblings, they were more likely to listen to him.

Brandon recalled a time when he was babysitting and couldn't find his brother. He said he searched everywhere and even got the neighbors to help. He was so afraid that the worst had happened and his brother was dead. He imagined how upset his mother would be, and believed he was to blame. Eventually he found his brother asleep under a bed; his brother thought it would be funny to hide from Brandon, and eventually fell asleep in his hiding spot. When Brandon found his brother, he was so upset and angry that he punched him. Brandon admitted that he still felt bad about doing that, but he also believed his brother deserved it.

Brandon's Answer of getting angry when he senses that someone he loves and is in charge of is in danger started at an early age. Because he was often in a state of overwhelm from too much responsibility, he also learned to believe that other people were the reason he felt so overwhelmed. And although that was true at the age of twelve, Brandon is now forty-five and a successful attorney. He now has the ability to handle things that he couldn't at the age of twelve. But when those early, overwhelming experiences are activated in the present, his anger is an automatic reaction. That reaction feels normal and understandable to Brandon. In order to help Brandon begin the EMDR process, we needed to address the concept of radical responsibility.

The first step for me was to make sure I really understood how getting angry when someone was hurt had been adaptive for Brandon. In response to his story about his experience at age twelve, I said, "Wow. You were in charge of four siblings at the age of twelve. I would imagine that being in charge of four children under the age of ten would be overwhelming for an adult at times, let alone a twelve-year-old." I continued, "That is pretty amazing that you were able to do that at that young age."

In response, Brandon looked at me and nodded. I was imagining a twelve-year-old boy frantically trying to find his brother and fearing that he was dead. In addition to the fear for his brother's life, Brandon also feared being blamed for any harm that came to his siblings. I went on, "As I imagine a twelve-year-old boy in that situation, I can see how anger was helpful. When you yelled at your siblings or they were afraid you might hurt them, it likely worked to get them to do what you wanted them to do." Brandon nodded again. I said, "As a twelve-year-old in charge of four younger siblings, this was likely the only tool you had to manage them." Because Brandon was not equipped for this responsibility, he was often in a state of fear and panic while he was in charge of his siblings. Fear and panic are very closely related to anger.

Once we understand the origin of our anger, or any other habit or issue we would like to change, we then have an opportunity to give ourselves compassion. Self-compassion helps us to release shame and guilt. Feelings of shame and guilt can be motivators to help us make changes in our lives, but if they persist without the means to make any necessary changes, it only serves to fuel problematic anger. Self-compassion can help us make the experience of shame or guilt a productive one, not an exercise in self-punishment.

The Dance with Circumstance

Unpleasant, hurtful, and annoying things happen in life. This will always be the case. You may even find yourself in a really awful situation that you had nothing to do with creating. Accidents happen, life events happen, world events happen, and we do not have control of many things. What we can control is our reaction to the uncontrollable things in life. What we can do is look at how we dance with our circumstance.

Once, when I was teaching SAFE EMDR to a group of mental health clinicians, one of the clinicians raised her hand and said, "What if the problem in your life is someone else and there is nothing you can do to change them?" I said, "In that case, we are looking at how you dance with the circumstance." Whatever the current situation or circumstance is, it is. There is nothing we can do to change the present moment. Imagine training for a marathon for a year and the day prior to the race, you are walking down the street and a bicycle comes up behind you and strikes you, resulting in a broken leg. It would be normal to feel disappointed and sad that you will not be able to run in the race. But no amount of hating your current situation is going to make it better. Actually, the longer you spend being angry and upset that your leg was broken by a careless bicyclist, the more stress chemicals you produce in your body. The more stress chemicals you produce in your body, the more inflammation your body produces. The more inflammation you have, the slower your leg will heal. Knowing that, wouldn't it be good to figure out a way to accept the current broken leg and focus on healing?

This sounds easy, but it takes practice. Accepting what is here is not about condoning what happened. It isn't even about forgiveness. It is about stopping the madness of wanting something to be here that isn't or wanting something to not be here that is. What currently is cannot be changed. The only thing we have the ability to change is the next moment. The best way to change the next moment is to stop wishing this moment was different than it is. Because by doing that, we are focusing on something that is impossible—changing what is. By accepting what is and looking at what we can do, we are empowering ourselves to change the only thing we have the ability to change—ourselves.

EXERCISE: Your Dance with Circumstance

Is any part of your problematic anger influenced by circumstances you don't have much control over? If so, or the next time you find yourself in an uncontrollable situation that causes suffering, consider how you might dance with the circumstance. What is it that you might need to accept in this situation, rather than hating it or wishing it were different? And—can you take responsibility for how you respond to it? Is there a way you participate in the pattern? What possibilities might open up if you do?

Take some time to write about this in your journal.

In this chapter, we have looked deeply at personal empowerment. You are powerless if you believe that your anger has been caused by something outside of you. With this view, change is not possible. If you are able to look inward to see how you are playing a part in the unhealthy patterns of your life, you are empowering yourself to make changes.

Chapter 8

Step Three: **Connecting the Present to the Past**

Why do you need to look at the past to resolve your anger? In my thirty years as a practicing clinician, no one has ever come into therapy saying they want to work on their childhood. People want to change because something isn't working in their current life and the root of the present issue is unclear to them. Many people know about events in childhood that were not great, but they believe it is in the past and no longer playing a role in their life. Even worse than that, they believe they had a great childhood and there is just something wrong with them that they are having problematic anger. Being willing and open to looking at how the past is manifesting in your system right now is an important step in the healing process.

Our memory networks help us learn and also connect us to the past. With SAFE EMDR, we are looking for the experiential root of anger. In the previous chapters, we've explored how anger is a problem across various areas in our lives. In this chapter, we will focus on how to find the experience that is in need of being updated or healed and is most likely a hidden fuel source for your problematic anger. The first step is to answer the question, "Are you ready to look deeply at the root of your anger?"

EXERCISE: Are You Ready?

Answering this question and taking the time to really listen to yourself and your body as you ask yourself this question is key. Are you willing to look deeply at the root of your anger in order to heal?

Feel free to write in a journal about your experience of asking yourself this question. Allow all parts of you to talk—the tension in your shoulders may have something to say, and that may be different than an open feeling in your heart or heaviness in your gut. Beginning to listen to yourself takes practice, but it is worth taking the time to do this.

You cannot go back in time. Whatever happened in the past is over. What we are doing with SAFE EMDR is finding the physical remnants of the past: the memories that have not fully processed that are currently fueling your problematic anger. We find those memories by looking at present-day experiences that activate a big emotional reaction, then we find the earlier memories that are the hidden source of pain. This is an important distinction, so I want you to hear it another way. As we look for the early, hurtful experience that has been left unprocessed in your system, we are not going back to the past. We are looking at how the past is continuing to manifest in this moment—how certain past experiences were left undigested in your brain and continue to fester like a hidden, unhealed wound. Every time an experience happens in the present that feels similar, you are bumping that unhealed wound. When that unhealed wound is activated, what comes up are the original emotions and physical sensations that happened earlier in life—sometimes much earlier. However, you are not aware that your current overreaction is about the past; it feels like it is about the present. When this happens, the way you see yourself and the world is clouded by the past experience, and you most likely think it is true.

You do not have to go back to the past to heal childhood wounds because the past is here, lying latent in your brain, unaware the past is over. This is the chapter that all of the other chapters have prepared you for, helping you understand and create conditions for this chapter to work for you.

SAFE EMDR is a type of therapy, and this is a self-help book. I will guide you to begin to look at how the past is connected to your current issues. However, doing EMDR therapy requires a trained mental health provider. This chapter will give you an idea of what to expect in the EMDR therapy process as you begin to connect with the past. If you have experienced multiple traumatic experiences or are currently experiencing psychiatric symptoms, you may want to skip some of the exercises. Even if you are not experiencing those things, there is a real benefit to having a mental health professional guiding you through the EMDR process.

One of the tools we will use in this chapter is SUD, Subjective Units of Distress. Similar to a pain scale, it is from 0 to 10, with 0 being not at all distressing and 10 being extreme distress. This is like a before-and-after picture that helps measure the progress you make in reprocessing memories. In the previous chapters, you had an opportunity to practice many resources. As you went through the exercises associated with nonviolence, mindfulness, compassionate assumption, and healthy boundaries, you were developing resources that will be very helpful in this chapter. Before you begin this chapter, I recommend that you practice one of those resources, or write down the most helpful ones and practice them prior to completing the exercises offered here. There are two important skills to have and practice prior to processing memories: the ability to intentionally go from upset to calmer, and the ability to recognize you are in this present moment as you experience the raw remnants of past events that feel like they are happening now. This dual awareness, one foot in the past and one foot in the present, is an important aspect of EMDR therapy.

Case Example: I Feel Like It Is Happening Now

David came to therapy for help with anger outbursts. He was a very successful businessperson who appeared calm in his professional life. However, with the people he was closest to, he often became violent and rageful. He was motivated to come to therapy by the threat of losing his family. As we linked his present-day anger to his past, David reported a childhood of severe neglect and a "relationship" with a friend's mother when he was a teenager. David had a lot of shame about the relationship, which started when he was fourteen and she was forty. Although he knew it was inappropriate, he didn't recognize the sexual abuse he endured. This abusive relationship lasted for a year, ending with a physical altercation with the abuser's husband. During the reprocessing eye movement phase, he buckled over and looked at me and said, "I feel like it is happening now." This is a good example of how sensory remnants of a memory can be left in a raw, unprocessed state in the brainstem. I looked him in the eye and said, "Yes, and it is not happening now; you are right here with me in my office, right?" My calm presence and the reminder that he was in my office and safe now helped him to tolerate reprocessing that difficult memory. The calm presence of an EMDR clinician is an important aspect of the EMDR therapy process, and can be very helpful to remind you that the past is over and you are just moving the material to a more adaptive place in your brain.

This recognition—that the past is manifesting in this moment in order to be healed—is an important aspect of SAFE EMDR. As I remained calm and reminded him that he is here now and safe, remembering what happened is an example of dual attention. David had experienced many flashbacks of his trauma, which is very different from what we are doing with EMDR therapy. The dual attention, one foot in the past and one foot in the present, is required for the memory to be reprocessed and for the activation to be released. The ability to know you are here in this moment remembering what happened is critical to successful healing in SAFE EMDR. That awareness can help you to tolerate the sensory remnants of the past as they surface and move to a more adaptive place in your brain.

In the eight phases of SAFE EMDR, the first two are the history taking and preparation phases. Those two phases were covered in previous chapters, where you looked at the history of your adaptations and strengths with the concept of The Answer, and as you explored resources, finding the problem and finding the early memories that are fueling problematic anger.

EXERCISE: Dual Attention

To practice dual attention, I would like to invite you to imagine a minor disturbance, a 4 or a 5 on the SUD scale of 0 to 10 and notice how you are feeling. If possible, notice the physical sensations you are having. Then I would like to invite you to use one of the resource exercises, like the deep breathing, grounding, or another useful exercise from the previous chapters, and notice if the disturbance shifts.

If you are able to go in and out of disturbance and know that what you are experiencing is a part of a memory, this is dual attention. You are able to mindfully notice the remnants of the past manifesting in your body through sensations, thoughts, and emotions, but also recognize it is in the past and you can use a resource to change your state. The more you practice mindful awareness, the more you can tolerate accessing the remnants of the past. As you are able to access these remnants with dual awareness, even if they are intense physical sensations or emotions, you are allowing those remnants to move to a more adaptive place in your brain. Recognizing that this is a physical process and real physical healing is happening can be a good motivator to allow whatever is here to be here.

Welcome Everything

Past unresolved experiences will often show up as physical sensations. Those sensations may be tightness in your abdomen, chest, or throat. It is important to welcome those sensations. If possible, notice those sensations and allow them. I once had a client who was very motivated to end the suffering she was experiencing as a result of past traumatic experiences that were not processed to an adaptive resolution. She asked me, "How do I get out of this pain?" I replied, "Welcome everything."

As you begin the process of accessing and releasing the remnants of the past in EMDR therapy, this may be very helpful for you to remember. Your system wants to heal. When you set the conditions for that healing to happen, whatever is in need of healing will surface. If you are able to welcome whatever is here, knowing that it is not happening now and allowing it to surface means you have a chance to transform the pain into peace.

When you are in EMDR therapy, it is important to remember that whatever comes up in phase four, reprocessing, is a part of a memory. Those memories are stored in a way that includes the disturbing experiences as well as the way you managed the experience at the time. Your Answer, your adaptive strength, is also an important thing to recognize and welcome.

For example, if you have a memory of being humiliated by a teacher at school when you were seven years old, as you begin accessing the memory, you may notice an urge to get up and go have a snack. Or you may notice an urge to call someone close to you. As you notice those urges or anything else that may come up to pull you out of the experience, can you tie that into the memory? Maybe having a snack was a way that you soothed yourself as a seven-year-old. It would be normal for a seven-year-old to want to call out to their parents or another safe adult when they are upset. These urges and responses come up with the memory because they are a part of the memory. This is one of the powerful ways that the concept of The Answer is important in the SAFE EMDR process.

Don't Believe Everything You Think

Jackie brought her four-year-old son in for therapy for behavior issues. She reported feeling exasperated by his behavior. He would often have meltdowns in public, which embarrassed and angered her. After talking to her and getting a history, it was clear that Jackie was having problematic anger responses to normal four-year-old behaviors. Jackie agreed to try SAFE EMDR for herself before getting treatment for her son.

Jackie lost her mother at an early age and was raised by her father. Her father would often drink too much, and his behavior embarrassed her. The target memory was when her father showed up drunk at her school play. As Jackie processed the memory of feeling responsible and embarrassed by her father's behavior, she naturally connected it with her anger and embarrassment with her son.

Jackie's Answer was to take on responsibility for the behavior of others. In her childhood, it was very helpful for her to be vigilant about the emotional state of her father. She wasn't as good at looking at her own emotions or tolerating other people having intense emotional responses. This continued as she brought her four-year-old in for treatment, not realizing that she was the one in need of help. Understanding her Answer and reprocessing the early memories helped Jackie to begin to change a lifelong pattern of codependence, frustration, and anger.

When memories are left unprocessed in raw form, they are also stored with the perception that you had at the time of the event. So if you are working on a memory from when you were very young, you will still have the perception of that age. You also may have the feeling that you cannot tolerate seeing the fragments of the memory surface. It is important to remember that you are now an adult and have developed many resources that you did not have at the time of the event. This is another way your Answer surfaces to try to help. If at the time of the memory, you zoned out or cut off emotionally from the experience, this may come up now alongside the memory. Seeing this as a part of the memory will help you to access and move it to a more adaptive place in your brain. The best way to do this is to say to yourself, "I wonder if that is what happened at the time?" This view of yourself will help you increase self-compassion and mitigate frustration, which may block the process.

Bilateral Practice

One unique aspect of EMDR is eye movements or bilateral stimulation. This is used for both accessing disturbing memories and for helping positive things feel more positive. You can use this aspect of the EMDR therapy on your own as you notice a mild disturbance. I would like to invite you to practice the bilateral stimulation techniques. I will offer several options for you to practice and you can choose which one works best for you. In EMDR therapy, the clinician will practice multiple ways of doing the bilateral movement so you will have options. I invite you to practice each type for approximately thirty seconds. In chapter 9, we will talk more about how they will be used in EMDR therapy to help lessen the disturbance of past experiences.

Knee tapping: Sitting with both feet on the floor and one hand on each knee, bring your hand up, one at a time, and land it on your knee, alternating sides like you are beating on a drum. Another option for this is to actually beat on a drum.

Side stepping: Standing up, begin stepping side to side. If you like, you can add in hand clapping.

Eye movement: Sitting in a chair, find two points in a room to help you move your eyes from side to side. You can also hold two fingers a few inches from your face and move your hand from side to side. The important thing in this method is that your eyes are crossing the centerline.

Butterfly hug: Cross your arms across your chest with hands holding on to the outside of each arm. Begin tapping your hands on your arms, or you can squeeze each arm alternately (Jarero and Artigas 2009).

Auditory plus tapping: Sitting at a table or desk, place your hands on the table about a foot out from the sides of your body. Hit down on the table hard enough to hear the sound of your hand hitting the table.

Finding the Targets

The process of finding the root of the present symptom is an important one. We are looking for the early memory that was not adequately digested in your brain, leaving it "hot." Like touching a live electrical wire, this amplifies your response to present-day situations. In chapter 6, you were invited to complete an exercise called How Is That a Problem? to help you uncover the ways that you are contributing to your symptom of problematic anger. In this chapter, you will be invited to look deeply at the experiences at the root of your anger in order to help those early memories move to a more adaptive place in your brain.

These early painful experiences are likely the things that you have been avoiding thinking about or remembering. These experiences are the reason you developed your Answers to help you cope with the pain of feeling unsafe or unloved, which is why self-compassion is so important in this process. No matter what you experience—even if you are unable to remember anything or just become numb—appreciating how that has been helpful will smooth the healing process.

There may be many distressing events in your life, but that does not mean you need to target all of them in your EMDR therapy. Even extremely disturbing experiences can be naturally processed through your brain to an adaptive place. We do this by talking about the event with a friend, journaling, dreaming, taking a walk, or doing other things that help us to process difficult experiences. Every disturbing event in your life does not need to be an EMDR target for reprocessing; only the ones that are dysfunctionally stored in your brain. The memory that is unprocessed is often a surprise to people and not something they may have "thought" was the root of their anger. Most of the time, we believe our reactions are only about things happening to us or outside of us.

Most people have ten to twenty unprocessed memories that contribute to most of the pain and suffering in their lives. A qualified EMDR clinician can be very helpful in helping you find these memories. The unprocessed remnants of these events become activated in the present via the raw pieces of the perceptions, emotions, and physical sensations that occurred at the time. Another way these memories surface is through the negative view you have about yourself or negative self-talk.

Negative Cognitions

The use of negative cognition in the EMDR process describes the feeling you have about yourself when you are at your worst. It is common that you "know better" and know that the negative belief isn't really true, but it feels true in certain situations. There are three categories of negative cognitions that reflect the past experience. Remember that these are irrational beliefs and not true. The reason it is helpful to find the negative cognition that accompanies your memory is the way the words help light up the memory, giving you access to it so you can release it. The negative belief you have about yourself as something happens in your life now can help you to find the early, unprocessed experience that is fueling your anger.

Here is a list of possible negative/positive cognitions:

Responsibility/Damaged or Defective	
I am bad	I am good
I am worthless	I am worthy/worthwhile
I'm not good enough	I'm fine as I am
I am shameful	I am honorable
I am damaged	I am whole
I don't matter	I am significant
Safety	
I cannot trust anyone	I can choose whom to trust
I am not safe	It's over, I'm safe now
I'm going to die	I'm alive
Lack of Control/Power	
I am powerless	I have choices now
My needs don't matter	I can choose what I want
I cannot trust myself	I can learn to trust myself
I have to be perfect	I'm okay as I am/It is okay to make mistakes
I can't handle it	I can handle it
I can't do it	I can choose to act

It's About You

The negative cognition is reflective of an irrational, negative belief you have about yourself that was developed as a result of an unprocessed memory remnant stored in your brain. It is important that the negative cognition you choose is about you, and not something that is true. It is also important that the belief is generalizable across various areas of your life. So for example, instead of "My mother didn't love me," it may be "I'm unlovable," and instead of "I'm a bad mother," it may be "I'm bad." Unfortunately, some mothers don't love their children and there are people who are bad mothers, so that can be true. But everyone is loveable, and no one is completely bad. The negative cognition that fits best will be used in the next chapter as we discuss the reprocessing phase of SAFE EMDR.

EXERCISE: The Memory Under The Answer

In this section, you will be guided by questions that are intended to light up different parts of your brain. The questions will help highlight the pathway from the present to the unprocessed memories that fuel your problematic anger. This is to give you an idea of what EMDR therapy is like. We always start with present frustrations or events that have been disturbing. In SAFE EMDR, we add in some ways to help you get under the adaptive response of your Answer. These questions will help you get under the anger to find the hurtful experiences that fuel it.

On a piece of paper, or using the worksheet from the online tools at http://www.newharbinger.com/54988, write down the answers to the following questions:

1. What is a current frustration or limitation? You are welcome to choose one from the How Is That a Problem? exercise in chapter 6 or come up with one here.
2. When you experience the above, what is the longing? What do you want in that moment that you are not getting?

3. Identify a recent time when you did have a hope, even a glimmer of hope, of that longing being fulfilled, but it didn't work out.
4. Use one of the bilateral methods as you notice the disturbance of this longing.

Example:

1. What is the current frustration? *I get frustrated because I have to do everything myself.*
2. When you experience the above, what is the relational longing? (This needs to be about what you want from others that you are not getting and not just about you.) *I wish the people close to me would support me. I long for someone to support me.*
3. What is a recent time when you did have a hope of that longing being fulfilled but it didn't work out? *I recently invited my sisters on a trip and thought we would finally get together and they all backed out at the last minute.*

Whatever you put as the recent incident will be the experience that you can use to find the early experience. By asking about the longing, we are looking beneath the surface to the early hurtful experience. This will be much more effective than just going with the frustration or anger that is protecting that experience. You are able to connect and be aware of the sadness, fear, or loss that may be the root of your problematic anger.

EXERCISE: Finding the Touchstone Memory

Francine Shapiro uses the term "Touchstone Memory" to describe the original hurtful experience that is inadequately processed (Shapiro 2017). Once you identify the most recent experience and the longing that goes with it, we have begun to activate the attachment wound. So in the example above, the present memory we would use to find the touchstone memory is the sisters backing out at the last minute.

In this exercise, you will have an opportunity to look at early experiences that may be fueling your problematic anger. This can help you have increased awareness of what is driving your anger. This is also a part of the EMDR therapy process. If you do not have childhood memories, it may be because it was helpful to shut those memories out. That doesn't mean you will not be able to benefit from EMDR therapy with a qualified therapist, but you may not be able to connect to those memories on your own.

If memories become too disturbing, you can stop or you can use a distancing technique, like imagining it happening as you watch it on a movie screen. It is also common to not have access to early memories if you have experienced a lot of overwhelming events in childhood. This doesn't mean EMDR will not work for you; it just means you may need more professional support prior to helping you through this process.

1. Concentrate on the memory that was upsetting and the relational longing. What is the most disturbing part of that experience right now?
2. What image represents the worst part of that memory?
3. What do you notice in your body?
4. When you bring up this memory, what negative thought goes with it?
5. On the SUD scale (0–10), how disturbing does it feel right now?
6. Notice the image, negative thought, and where you feel it in your body, then let your mind go back to the earliest time you felt similar.
7. Is there an earlier time?
8. Is there an earlier time? (Keep asking yourself this question until there are no earlier times.)

9. Write down the early memories on a sheet of paper.
10. Use one of the resources, like breathing shift, grounding, or another resource you practiced, to help you release the activation and get to a calmer state.

Memories and Lies

One result of unprocessed memories is a negative view of how you see yourself or your place in the world. In SAFE EMDR we have a chart called Memories and Lies. I have a belief that anything that keeps you from being a shining star is either a memory or a lie. Being a shining star is being your authentic self, freely giving and receiving love and offering your unique gifts to the world. Any way you are blocked or restricted from that is due to "Memories" that are left unprocessed, and the accompanied "Lies" that are the limiting negative beliefs or the conclusions you made about yourself as a result of your distressing experiences.

You can use the Memories and Lies chart to help you keep track of current life triggers, the connections to the past, the negative beliefs that goes along with them, and what is new and true. Here is an example:

Date/Time: 10/15 @ 2:00 p.m.

What was your experience? My friend canceled our dinner.

SUD (0-10): 7

What was the memory or lie? I'm not good enough. Memory of my siblings teasing me.

What is New and True? I'm fine as I am, the past is over, and my friend was overwhelmed at work and had to cancel.

What resources can you use? I can meditate to calm down and call another friend.

Using this chart when you are upset about something will help you remember that it is the past being activated and remind you of your resources. There is also a worksheet version of this chart in the online tools at http://www.newharbinger.com/54988.

Summary

In this chapter, you made the decision to look deeply at the root of your anger. You tested out your ability to go from upset to calm. You decided on a current issue to work on, and found the longing and early memories associated with that issue. You also had several opportunities to practice using the resources you developed in the other chapters. In the next chapter, we will discuss examples of EMDR therapy reprocessing. We will also give you some examples of how you can use aspects of EMDR on your own.

Chapter 9

Step Four: Releasing the Emotional Charge of Past Experiences

In this chapter, I will discuss how to activate and release the emotional charge of past experiences. While it is not possible to do psychotherapy on yourself, this chapter will outline some self-help ways of connecting to and releasing some of the charge of past, unresolved wounds. While understanding the origin of your anger can help you gain insight, insight isn't the same as releasing. This chapter may also give you hope of finally releasing the fragments of past negative experiences. Relinquishing those stuck fragments can help you reduce your reactivity to triggers and live a more peaceful life in the present.

EMDR is an eight-phase psychotherapy approach. Millions of people have achieved healing from experiencing this therapy. Phase four, the reprocessing phase, is the part most people consider to be EMDR, but all eight phases are required to most effectively utilize the therapeutic approach. Reprocessing happens best when the other phases are adequately completed. Phases one and two, the history taking and preparation phases, are crucial in preparing and making the best treatment plan. In those first two phases, the clinician is gathering historical information as well as the client's current resources and what they need for optimal success in the EMDR process. Another part of the first two phases is ensuring the client remains safe throughout the treatment.

With SAFE EMDR, we do this by using the concept of The Answer. We spend time exploring how present symptoms may be adaptive, or reflect past behaviors or perspectives that were previously helpful. We do this very intentionally with a sense of appreciation for how someone dealing with problematic anger managed to survive some very difficult and often painful situations. We address these adaptations first because they are what will stand in the way of accessing the pain of the past. By looking at the strategies you developed to protect yourself and appreciating how they helped in the past, you are preparing a smooth path to healing problematic anger.

In formal EMDR, in addition to current symptoms or Answers, we also explore how the client managed in the past. For example, if someone experienced a lot of trauma and ongoing stress in their youth, using drugs and/or alcohol was likely something that they found helpful. Even if they are currently clean and sober, we want to explore these past Answers in order to best prepare the client for safe and effective EMDR therapy reprocessing. This is important because when we access the stuck memory fragments of early experiences, urges for those unhealthy ways of managing may also arise. This doesn't always happen, but we want to predict and prepare for the worst. So if you have a history of unhealthy coping mechanisms, it is important that you are honest with yourself about those things. If you are engaging in EMDR therapy with a professional, you need to be honest and open about any dangerous coping mechanisms you have previously used. If you are not engaging in EMDR therapy, be prepared in the event that previous coping strategies surface as you look back on past, painful experiences. For example, if you predict that urges to use alcohol or substances will come up, it gives you an opportunity to make a plan to use healthier coping strategies, which may be as simple as asking a trusted friend to be available to you if needed.

Adverse Childhood Experiences Study

There is a research study that was conducted by Kaiser Permanente and the Centers for Disease Control and Prevention that looked at negative experiences in childhood and the risk of developing chronic health conditions, high-risk health behaviors, low quality of life, and early death. The ACEs (Adverse Childhood Experiences) questionnaire had ten questions regarding physical and sexual abuse, neglect, and experiences of loss through divorce or death, mental illness in the family, and having a family member go to prison. They found that if a person replied yes to four or more of the ten questions, they were at much higher risk of chronic health issues, mental health issues, and substance abuse issues.

I share this information to point out that people who experienced a highly stressful childhood often find short-term relief through things like smoking, drinking, or drugs. They are also more likely to have depression, anxiety, and suicidal thoughts or attempts. Adults who experienced this often feel guilt or shame about things they did as a child or teenager. This study demonstrated that children from highly stressful homes have the deck stacked against them, and it is understandable that they used what worked to help them get through their childhood. If this was the case for you, self-compassion may be very helpful. Another reason I bring attention to this study is, if you experienced a highly stressful childhood and have a history of substance abuse or suicidal thoughts or actions, it is important that you have a specific plan in place prior to doing EMDR reprocessing. Although you may not experience urges to use or suicidal thoughts, having a plan in place if they do surface is the best course of action.

Dissociation as an "Answer"

When faced with overwhelming stress or potentially life-threatening situations, humans have a built-in system to cope: dissociation. We all dissociate to some degree, from zoning out to the experience of leaving your body and being completely cut off from emotions. When someone experiences chronic trauma in childhood, dissociation may be the only tool they have to survive. People who frequently dissociate may have difficulty accessing and successfully processing early memories with EMDR prior to doing some important work in phase two, the preparation phase of EMDR. Trauma can disrupt a child's natural emotional regulation, leading to difficulties managing emotions as an adult. Young children coregulate their emotions with a safe adult, but if they have an abusive caregiver, they may automatically dissociate, cutting off from their emotions and at times their physical body. It is common for those children to resort to other dissociation strategies as adults, like using alcohol and drugs, picking skin or cutting, over- or undereating, gambling, sex addiction, or other addictions. These strategies may be the only way a person currently manages emotions.

A qualified EMDR professional can help you develop healthy ways to tolerate and manage emotions. Toxic shame is often a result of trauma and can be a barrier to getting adequate help for the results of trauma (Dolezal and Gibson 2022). Letting go of toxic shame and giving yourself compassionate understanding is very helpful in releasing old patterns and developing new ones. The first step is seeing the shame as a protective, adaptive response and not as a sign that you are defective in some way.

A Case Example

Amanda was a refugee from a war-torn country who experienced extreme neglect and abuse as a child. She came into therapy to help with experiences of what she called "blind rage." During these rage episodes, which were frequently triggered by alcohol consumption, she felt out of control and unable to pull herself out of it. She often couldn't remember everything that had happened and felt a lot of shame when she later realized the aftermath of her behavior. This is an example of dissociation. The trauma that Amanda experienced as a child was overwhelming and she didn't have an adult to help her manage the overwhelm. Dissociation was all she had until she discovered alcohol as a young teen. Although the alcohol seemed to be effective in regulating her emotions at first, it progressed to a dangerous level. Amanda would often drink to excess and experience blackouts.

Although Amanda could remember some traumatic events from her childhood, it was important for us to take the time to help her practice some resources to help her regulate and tolerate her emotions without using any substances prior to reprocessing those memories. It was a very gradual process, but she was very motivated, and was able to progressively become more skilled at tolerating and managing her emotional state. After she was able to demonstrate and practice skills that helped her to gain healthy coping skills, we were able to successfully complete the reprocessing phase of EMDR.

Practicing Being Present

Dissociation is a way of managing difficult experiences by cutting off from your body and self in some way. Understanding and becoming aware of ways that you cut off in small ways can be helpful. Once you are aware, you can use that awareness to practice being present. Each time you notice the habit of going away and choose to bring yourself back, you are expanding your ability to be present. Some ways to practice being present are:

- Notice your breath going all the way in and all the way out.
- Notice the bottom of your feet on the floor. Experiment with pushing your feet into the floor to see if you feel more present.
- Put your hand in cold water or eat an ice cube.
- Smell something strong like vanilla extract or peppermint.

What to Expect with Reprocessing Memories

Directly addressing early disturbing memories with EMDR reprocessing can look different for different people. This will depend on how the memory is stored and which fragments of that memory are still "hot." The best way to approach the reprocessing phase is to be open to whatever is here and allow the fragments to surface. In my thirty years of experience as an EMDR clinician, no two people have had the same experience. With successful EMDR reprocessing, whatever is stuck will surface if the conditions of safety and preparation have been adequately addressed.

It can be a paradigm shift to begin to welcome and become curious about the disturbing memories you access. Most people have spent a lifetime trying to avoid thinking about those things. As you begin to experience EMDR reprocessing for the first time, a trusting relationship with a trained clinician will go a long way to helping you heal. For example, the clinician can help keep a calm presence, what's called coregulation in therapy. When you are with a trusted person who is calm and present, your nervous system can sense that presence. Coregulation is the way we all regulate our nervous system as babies. It is also very helpful as an adult.

As you are doing the reprocessing phase, you will start with one specific memory. If it is the comprehensive EMDR therapy protocol, you will ideally start with the early memory you found, your Touchstone Memory. Throughout the reprocessing phase, that is the memory that you will be rating from 0 to 10. In the EMDR reprocessing phase, we target one memory at a time.

Like I mentioned, there are eight phases to EMDR therapy. Phase three is very short and always done only with phase four. The purpose of phase three is to light up the way the memory is stored in the system and to get a baseline measurement of how disturbing the memory feels prior to the eye movement or other bilateral movement in phase four.

Once you and the clinician light up the memory in phase three, what should you expect with the phase four reprocessing? Like I said earlier, the best way to get through this phase is to be open and curious about anything that happens. It is very common that the dysfunctionally stored fragments of memory cause a physical sensation. If you are able to notice that sensation and not be afraid of it, you will have more success in releasing the disturbance.

A Case Example

Joe came into therapy to try to save his marriage. He had recently discovered that his wife had a brief affair several years ago, and reported feeling obsessed with thoughts of hurting the other person and severe anger outbursts since finding out. He stated that he recognized his part in the problems in his relationship—that he had difficulty trusting people and often felt suffocated in relationships. He described himself as a workaholic, and that when he wasn't working, he spent his time focused on dirt bike racing and working on his bike.

Joe was the youngest of seven children in a very poor family. He described his father as a mean alcoholic, while his mother was often depressed and spent days in bed. He was often left alone at a young age with his siblings, where he was often targeted by them in various ways due to being the youngest. It is normal for children who are experiencing a stressful, traumatic life to be physically aggressive toward other children.

I was curious about the way Joe described his present issue of difficulty trusting and feeling suffocated. As we completed the treatment plan, we found a touchstone memory when Joe was four years old and his brothers talked him into getting into a toy box that had a lid on it. Once he got in, the brothers sat on the lid and wouldn't let him out. The negative cognition Joe reported was "I'm stupid." This negative cognition also resonated with how he felt when he found out about his wife's affair. We used that memory as his first target for EMDR reprocessing.

In the free online tools for this book at http://www.newharbinger.com/54988, you can find a full account of Joe's EMDR therapy experience, going through phases 3–8 of the EMDR process for that particular memory.

Help When Stuck

As was the case with Joe, many people are able to easily release the emotional charge of the past without a lot of intervention from the clinician. However, there are times that clients get stuck in phase four and need more guidance and intervention. A properly trained EMDR therapist will have many tools to help keep the process moving.

Sometimes people experience difficulty with reprocessing when the memory is too disturbing and they struggle to maintain present-moment awareness. When this happens, the clinician may offer a way to help the client distance from that memory. They may say something like, "You're here in my office now, right? It isn't happening now." If that doesn't work, they may offer a metaphor for the client to use. They may say something like, "Would you like to imagine that you are watching the memory like a movie up on a screen?" Sometimes they may suggest that the client imagine that a known, supportive figure or person is sitting next to them, holding their hand and watching it with them. In Francine Shapiro's book *Getting Past Your Past*, she suggests imagining the scene as a cartoon and that things are happening with a funny cartoon voice (2013).

The Answer concept is another tool to help when someone is stuck in the reprocessing phase. Since our Answers are developed to help us manage difficult situations, predicting that they will surface in the reprocessing phase is very helpful. For example, if someone has a history of rescuing people and is really good at noticing how other people are feeling, they may notice suddenly being worried about someone while reprocessing a memory. They may become concerned about taking up time in a session or become worried about me in some way. As a clinician, I am always thinking about how everything ties back into the memory. When that happens, I usually say something like, "I wonder if that happened at the time?" This is usually helpful for the person to connect the current behavior to the early memory. When it comes to overcoming blocks in the reprocessing phase of EMDR, both predicting the blocks will happen and assuming the block was once helpful can be very useful.

Outside of therapy, practicing using the concept of The Answer toward yourself can help you reduce shame and increase self-compassion. You can use this when you have a negative emotional response toward yourself as you remember a painful childhood experience. Just saying to yourself, "I wonder if this is what happened at the time?" or

"I wonder how this was helpful to me at the time?" can begin to change lifelong patterns that keep problematic anger charged.

Appreciating and Releasing

As you have worked through this book, you may have automatically connected to some early childhood memories that appear to be related to your problematic anger. Your past experiences become a part of your story. The negative belief you adopted as a result of those experiences keeps the story alive and often limits you unnecessarily. It is possible to update that story. The following exercises may help you connect more to the vulnerable, hurt part of you that your Answer has been trying to protect. It also may connect you to painful memories and even memories you didn't previously have access to. While the following exercises are not EMDR therapy, I have found them helpful in releasing some of the excess charge of the past.

A Thank-You Note to Your Answer

I would like to invite you to write a thank you note to your Answer. Your Answer developed to keep you safe and connected. It is important to appreciate your Answer and also let that part of you know that things have changed. As you write to your Answer, it may be helpful to let your Answer know what has changed since you were young. When doing this, it can be helpful to imagine the younger you who had to adapt to difficult situations and let that younger you know that you are older and have other options now. For example, start with anger as an Answer. Can you appreciate how your anger began as a way to protect you? What part of your life was that anger trying to protect?

Journaling and Bilateral Stimulation

If you have identified an early memory that is not too overwhelming, it can be helpful to journal about that early experience. While journaling you can use alternative feet tapping or you can listen to bilateral music on headphones. There are several options for bilateral music that can be found online. Start writing about the story, the worst part, the irrational belief you have, the emotion, and the body sensations. If possible, allow the story to naturally unfold as you write. Any time the story feels too overwhelming, stop and use one of the resources we discussed. Just stopping and noticing your breath can be helpful. At the end of the story, it can be very helpful to write about what is new and true. Write about your new positive belief, new resources, and positive relationships you have now. Remind yourself that the past is over and you have survived it. You may want to write about all of the positive ways your life has changed since that time. Letting the younger you know that you have many more skills, choices, and resources now. You are much more able to protect and care for yourself now. As much as possible, give yourself words of appreciation and love.

Chapter 10

Step Five: **A New Peaceful Path**

If you want to have the most comprehensive results with EMDR, it is important to take the time to decide what you want. Most of us are really good at knowing what we *don't* want. When people come in for psychotherapy, they have "problems" in their life and they just want those problems to stop. Pain is a great motivator for change; most of us just want to be out of pain. However, if you have a habit or problematic anger or anything else, another habit needs to replace the one you stop. That habit will form either intentionally or unintentionally. We are always changing; the more we can be intentional about the direction we want that change to take, the better. Being intentional about the new patterns you want in your life is the best way to create a life you would like to have.

Your Future Desired Life

When you engage in EMDR therapy, it is common to start with the earliest memories related to your problematic anger. By reprocessing the earliest memories first, you are clearing the way for creating a more intentional life that you desire. After all of the stuck fragments of the past are freed from your system, you should notice a big difference in your reactivity in your present life. Ideally, the next step is to begin to imagine how you would like to be in the future.

In EMDR therapy, we look at the past, present, and future. As we do this, we are really just looking at right now. In the case of problematic anger, we are looking at how the past experiences are still fueling your anger, what recent things in the present trigger your anger, and how you would like to respond, feel, or react in the future when something similar happens. I find it very helpful to remember that all we can experience is now. As we are experiencing now, we can recognize how the fragments of the past are creating an overreaction to the present. In the present, we can recognize how the outside world and events trigger our past, undigested experiences. As we think about how we would like to be in the future, we imagine ourselves in similar situations in the future in which we would normally be triggered into anger. As we imagine those times, we think about how we would like to react, feel, or believe when those things happen, instead of reacting with anger. This is how EMDR addresses all aspects of the memory system.

Imagining the future is very much related to our past experiences. What we believe is possible is related to what we have already experienced. That is why it can be helpful to stretch yourself by imagining your wildest dreams first. Starting with slightly unrealistic dreams is often easiest because you feel less pressure to immediately achieve them. For some people, thinking about what they want creates pressure to actually go out and do those things.

I would like to encourage you to make this chapter as playful as possible. It is less about making a plan or setting a goal than it is about practicing a different way of thinking.

Learning to Dream

As you think about the concept of The Answer, it is understandable that some people are more familiar with what they want than others. If you grew up in a family where you were on your own a lot, you may have had lots of practice at making decisions and knowing what you want. You are also likely good at being resourceful and can figure out unique ways to problem solve. But if you grew up in a situation where it was dangerous or unwelcome to speak up and ask for what you wanted, you likely have a harder time deciding what you want. So if you struggle with this section, be kind to yourself and know that the more you practice dreaming, the better you will get at it.

About thirty years ago, I started keeping a "Dreams List" file. It is a very simple exercise, just making a list of dreams. Now, you'll do the same for yourself. I recommend that you don't put too much thought into the things you write down. This is not a to-do list; you will not be obligated to achieve the things you put on the list. It is more about exercising your ability to know what you want. While you may not actually ever buy the oceanside mansion, this will tell you something about what you would like more of in your life. Maybe your soul craves more solitude and nature; that wish may be fulfilled by visiting a local park, walking in the woods, or fishing in a local lake. So dream big—it will point you in the right direction.

EXERCISE: Dreams List

What if you had no limits? Can you imagine having no limits of talent, time, support from others, money, or any other limits?

What would you do or experience?

Where would you go?

What would you create?

What would you accomplish?

How would you give back?

Make a list of twenty things in your journal.

Here are some examples that may help inspire you. Feel free to use any of these if they resonate with you, or go way beyond them. It is *your* dreams list.

- Walk the Appalachian Trail
- Buy an RV and travel across the country
- Visit all of the US National Parks
- Develop a school that helps children in poverty
- Go on a month-long vacation with my best friend
- Pay off all my debt
- Finish my high school diploma

- Write a book about my childhood
- Interview Michael Jordan
- Drive an Indy 500 race car
- Spend a week alone in a tent in the woods
- Develop a regular fitness routine and get in shape
- Pay off my parents' home and debt
- Run a marathon
- Get a job working for Google
- Attend a meditation retreat
- Buy a Roush Mustang
- Go on an African safari
- Learn to play the guitar
- Have frequent gatherings with my family and friends

I suggest that you keep your dreams list in a file. If this is a really difficult exercise, you may want to create a dreams list daily or weekly. Just like anything else, practicing something helps you get better at it. Since I started my dreams list thirty years ago, it is a paper file, but you can create one on your computer or smartphone.

In my experience of creating these lists, I have found that, over the years, many of the things on my list have come to be. This is without consciously doing anything other than making the list, without setting any goals or objectives. At the time I was making the list, I felt like the things on my list were wild dreams. But they happened. Of course, some of the things on my list didn't happen, but as I look back at those items, I realize that they would not be on my dreams list today.

If you took the time to create your dreams list, I would like to invite you to look at the items on it. Is there a pattern to your dreams? Do many of them have a similar theme? For example, are many of them about places you want to travel? Are many of them experiences you want to have with important people in your life? Or are they about things you want to have in your life? Looking at the patterns can help you see what you are lacking in your life. Maybe you don't have the time or money to take a trip to Paris, but you could make a plan to meet a friend at a French cafe or restaurant.

Creating a Collage

If you are a very visual person, creating a collage or a vision board is a great way to practice deciding what you want in your life. This activity can be done by cutting out photos from magazines and gluing them on a piece of cardboard, or it can be done online. It can be helpful to begin this process with an intention. Your intention is up to you; it can be a global intention, like creating a happy, fulfilling life, or it could be something more specific. You could create a collage about how you would like to feel in your career, love life, family life, or socially. You could also create a collage about an area of your future.

Transitions and Opportunities

Life has many transitions. Things are always ending and new opportunities are on the other side of the endings. Recognizing and planning for these transitions can be a powerful way to intentionally imagine your desired future. Sometimes we avoid recognizing endings because we don't want to feel the loss of something. I remember when I was a senior in high school many, many years ago. My friends and I were talking to a teacher about what we were doing after graduation. We told him that we planned to stay in touch and visit each other at our different colleges. He said, "You think you will keep in touch, but you probably won't." That was in 1979, and we didn't have social media or even email back then. Staying in touch relied on letters or expensive long-distance phone calls. Although we tried, eventually my friends and I drifted apart.

As I remember that time, I realize that our promises to stay in touch may have been a way to avoid the pain of leaving each other. There's nothing wrong with what we did, but if I could go back in time and do things differently, I would intentionally recognize the transition. I would invite my friends to gather and talk about our memories. It would be kind of like a funeral or celebration of the life of our childhood. Even if my friends and I did stay in touch after we left high school, there was no denying that things were about to change.

How we deal with change is often a reflection of our past experiences with loss and unpredictability. If you have experienced early loss or abandonment, you may have difficulty saying goodbye or acknowledging loss. Painful past experiences can drive people to skip over recognizing the ending and move directly to something new. With relationships, this can have negative effects. By not taking time to grieve the loss of a relationship, we lose the chance to heal and move forward in a more conscious manner. By recognizing a time of transition, you have an opportunity to learn from the past and be conscious of what you would like to manifest for the future. If you have a pattern of avoiding goodbyes or recognizing loss, this may be a new experience for you.

Here are some examples of opportunities to recognize transitions:

- Moving to a new home
- Changing jobs
- Children moving out
- Divorce or relationship losses
- Death of friends or family members
- Milestone birthdays
- Anniversaries
- Completion of a large project
- Closing a business
- Changing directions in a career

Feel free to take some time to write in your journal about any recent transitions you have experienced or possibly have coming up in the near future. Is there a way you can acknowledge the ending? It may be helpful for you to write about what you have learned and how you are feeling. Taking the time to reflect on this may help you make space to examine what you would like the future to hold for you.

EXERCISE: The Future Movie

Begin by thinking about a time in the recent past when you were triggered and angry. In EMDR therapy we call these "present triggers." I recommend that you choose something that is mild, like a 3 or 4 on a scale of 0 to 10.

It is important that you bring up something specific that you can see happening and not just a general issue. For example, instead of "getting angry about the news," it would be "seeing my friend's political post on social media yesterday." It is important too that you choose an actual memory, because then you will know what changes as you recall that memory again.

From there, establish the future response that you would *like* to have when this situation, or one like it, arises in the future. After that, consider: what is the positive belief that your future desired adaptive response represents?

Once you've established that, you'll be ready to "run the movie." This means to imagine, as vividly as you can, yourself practicing your future desired response to the present trigger. It means to imagine yourself really acting on the positive belief you wish to hold, in place of the beliefs and instincts that drive your problematic anger. Then, you'll consider how you feel, watching the movie you've made for yourself. That will help you strengthen the patterns of adaptive, productive behavior you wish to practice. It will also help you deal with any of the unprocessed feelings that may otherwise drive you back to triggered, anger-filled responses.

Here is an example:

Present Trigger: Reading a friend's political social media post and becoming angry.

Future Desired Response: I would like to remain calm, get off of the social media thread, and go do something relaxing, like listening to my favorite music.

Positive Belief: I have choices.

Begin slow bilateral movements—tapping, alternate arm squeezing, and the like, as described in chapter 8.

Running the movie along with the words "I have choices": "Imagining myself seeing the social media post, taking a deep breath, and walking away from my device. I walk into my living room and turn on some classical music and begin noticing my body relaxing. I remind myself that it is okay to not engage with people on social media and even give myself permission to take a break from it. I see myself relaxing and enjoying the music. I notice that I am even beginning to smile and feel happy. I know that it is okay to set boundaries for myself and it is important for me to take care of myself."

If you notice feeling more positive: Feel free to repeat the above movie and add in any further positive things that came up.

If you notice feeling neutral: You may want to write in your journal more about how you would like to feel, believe, and respond instead of the recent experience. Take time to notice and write about how you would like to feel in more detail. Repeat the above.

If you notice feeling negative: Notice the negative emotion experience. If it feels tolerable, repeat the above with the positive statement. Any time you feel the need to stop, do so and use one of the calming resources in the previous chapters.

Let's try the practice.

Choose a recent time you became mildly angry.

Now imagine how you would like to feel, react, or believe if a similar situation happens in the future. Write about the new positive experience in your journal. Use as much visual detail as possible as you write about your desired future response.

What positive words about yourself would you like to believe when something similar happens in the future? (Examples: "I can handle it." "I am fine." "I am safe." "I am calm and confident.") Feel free to come up with your own positive belief that resonates with you. Write your positive belief down in your journal.

Now I would like to invite you to bring up your positive belief and begin imagining yourself doing the new positive experience as if you were watching yourself in a movie. Try to have a beginning, middle, and end. As you are running the movie, add in some bilateral tapping of your choice.

If you feel your movie became more positive, run it again. Keep repeating until you feel complete.

If you had negative feelings while running the movie, you have two choices:

> Run the movie again and see if it improves.
>
> Stop and move to the next section of the book, Filling in the Blanks.

If you felt nothing as you ran the movie, you have choices:

> Run the movie again, and this time, speak it out loud as you do tapping.
>
> Write the story down. Use details about how you would like to feel, believe, and react. Read it out loud as you do tapping.

Filling in the Blanks

If you had only negative feelings with the last exercise of running a movie, there may be a few different reasons for that. The first reason may be that you picked a recent triggering experience that was too big. Although this exercise can be effective without resolving all of your past, stuck, disturbing memories, at times they can block the process. So if you haven't engaged in EMDR therapy, you may want to consider it. Ideally, addressing your future desired life is best done after the past has been adequately resolved.

Another reason some people have difficulty running the future movie is due to necessary skills, talents, or experiences that need to be developed. If you have had many years of problematic anger, you may have a difficult time even imagining feeling calm and confident. You also may have a difficult time imagining yourself doing anything other than your old patterns that are fueled by anger.

If you had difficulty with the previous exercises, this one may help you begin. If you didn't have trouble with the previous exercises, this exercise can be helpful to see a direction to take.

EXERCISE: Filling in the Blanks

Taking a step in the direction of the life you desire can be a very powerful experience. Review the Dreams List and The Future Movie exercises and see if you are noticing any patterns. For this exercise, I would like you to consider what "baby steps" may look like as you begin the journey to break these patterns and walk a more peaceful path. I encourage you to use your journal to write down the answers to these prompts. I also encourage you to answer these questions quickly, without putting a lot of thought into it. You are not committing to a contract; you are expanding the way you think. (For a worksheet version of this exercise, see the online tools at http://www.newharbinger.com/54988.)

1. A place I feel most at peace is ______________.
2. A place I love to go is ______________.
3. I feel most like myself when I am ______________.
4. When I was a kid, I loved ______________.
5. The subject I liked most in school was ______________.
6. When I have free time, I like to ______________.
7. Something I would love to learn about is ______________.
8. My ideal environment is ______________.
9. If it were easy, I would ______________.

10. My ideal day is ________________.
11. Time moves most quickly when I am ________________.
12. If it were only up to me, I would ________________.
13. If I weren't afraid, I would ________________.
14. I feel most safe when I am ________________.
15. I feel most loved when I am ________________.

Now I would like to invite you to look over the answers to this and the other exercises in this chapter.

Do you see any patterns?

As you look through your responses, do you light up with some of them more than others?

What tiny steps can you take to bring more of what you want into your life? Take a moment to write about this in your journal.

Chapter 11

A Plan for Ongoing Guidance and Support

As you have moved through this book, some of you may have been working with a trained EMDR professional along the way. If so, I hope this book has helped you to navigate that process a little more smoothly. If you have been reading this book and not in therapy, hopefully you were able to increase your awareness of how past, unhealed wounds may be feeding problematic anger.

This book has offered a slightly different view of the EMDR process with the SAFE EMDR approach. The principles and exercises in this book are intended to help you navigate through the EMDR process in a smooth and kind manner.

It can be helpful to find a way to reinforce the things you have learned in this book. I would like to give you a few "takeaways" to help you keep moving toward a more peaceful way of living. I will offer a statement for each area and, if what I offer here doesn't resonate with you, feel free to create your own statement. It may be helpful to write the statements down and post them in a place where you can easily see them.

Big Picture Things to Remember

The past is over.

Anything that keeps you from knowing you are a shining star is a memory or a lie. If you can recognize that the past is over, you can be free of it. We are all dragging the past around with us. We drag it around in the form of unprocessed, negative memories and beliefs about ourselves. Releasing those fragments of the past can help you be less reactive and fully enjoy the present.

Your anger has been helpful.

It may be difficult to grasp, but appreciating the helpful nature of your anger is the fastest way to be free of it. Your anger was developed as a defense. It was an attempt to protect you when you needed it. It can be helpful to imagine the younger you who needed anger for protection. You can let that younger you know the past is over. You can also let that part of you know that you have new, more peaceful ways to take care of yourself now.

Our reactions are internal.

No matter what happens outside of you, your reaction is internal. This may seem obvious, but it is important to remember. If you remember this, you can become curious about the unhealed remnants of the past that are still hanging around. Becoming curious about how the past is showing up now is a way to empower yourself. Recognizing that your reaction is within you also gives you a chance to use one of your calming tools to help you change your emotional state.

Continuing to Work with Your Answer

Throughout this book, you have been invited to look within to see your patterns. Prior to hearing about the concept of The Answer, you may not have had awareness of these patterns. Most of our patterns are unconscious and just feel like normal life. If you have started to see how the concept of The Answer applies to you, that is a great start. If you can see your patterns of connection and protection appearing, it is an opportunity to make different choices, or at least appreciate the adaptive origin of your response. This is a difficult task, but if you are committed to personal growth, just noticing and appreciating your Answer can be very helpful.

If you want to begin to have more self-awareness, the concept of the Answer is a simple tool to help you with that. Our Answers are:

- The patterns we developed to maximize connection and protection
- Our greatest strength
- Our automatic, patterned way of dealing with stress
- The way we sabotage ourselves
- The way we stay engaged in old patterns that we would like to stop
- Often what feels like the only option as a response

Take a moment here to think about your Answer. It may be helpful to write about it in your journal. Imagine yourself as a child and how you developed your Answer to help you. It may be helpful to write directly to that child. You can review chapter 5 if needed.

Important aspects of noticing and working with your Answer:

- Appreciate that your Answer developed to help you when you needed it.
- When you become frustrated by your Answer, it can be helpful to imagine yourself as a child and appreciate that you found something that helped you when you were hurting.
- Your Answer developed because you needed something that you didn't get or you got something that you didn't want. Try to connect with that need and find a way to give it to yourself. (Example: You needed someone to tell you that you matter and your feelings matter.) Tell that to yourself and remind yourself that you are able to give yourself what you need now.

Embodying the Principles

The SAFE EMDR principles are foundational for a more peaceful, harmonious life. Once you begin to embody these principles, you will find that you are experiencing less resentment, frustration, and anger, and more peace. Here are some tips for adding these principles to your life.

Nonviolence Toward Yourself

"I accept that I cannot change the past. I am willing to be kind to myself in order to become a kinder, more peaceful person."

Where is your anger? Is it outside of you or inside of you? Taking a nonviolent approach toward yourself is a shift from self-loathing to self-compassion. Being kind to yourself is not about making excuses but about offering yourself a new way of reacting to your anger, and extinguishing its fuel source. It is likely that hating and shaming yourself with hurtful self-talk is actually fueling your problematic anger and not healing it.

By recognizing anger as an Answer, you are seeing how it developed to help keep you safe or connected in your early years of life. You are making a nonviolent shift in your relationship with yourself.

Guilt and shame only serve to help you change your behavior. If you are feeling guilt and shame, it may be helpful to make a plan for how you can do something different in the future. If you are having difficulty making changes, an EMDR clinician can be very helpful as a support.

Nonviolence Toward Others

"I release the need to judge others. I choose to use my energy in positive, peaceful ways."

You cannot change anyone but yourself. Allowing the outside world to have the power to trigger your anger is giving others the power to control your emotional state. This is especially true when it comes to things you look at in the news and social media.

- Would you like to have more control over what you allow in your life and what you do not?
- Would you like it if you could release the need to be "right"?
- Would you like to spend your energy on things that matter to you instead of things that trigger anger?

Some things may seem harmless but can reinforce old angry patterns. Gossip may seem harmless, but it can fuel anger. It is likely the person you are talking about will never hear what you are saying. However, gossip is often negative and reflects a judgmental mindset. If you gossip about others, you are practicing negativity and judgment. Here are some ways to get out of judgmental, gossipy conversations—say:

- "I'm trying to focus on positive things that I can do something about. I find it helps me feel more peaceful and happy."
- "I try to not problem solve for other people without being asked."
- "I'm on a thirty-day gossip cleanse, so I have nothing to add."

Mindful Awareness

"I recognize that my experience is a perception based on body sensations, thoughts, and emotions. I can notice my experience and be curious about it."

The intention to increase your mindful awareness is a step in the direction of decreasing problematic anger. Chronic anger reactions are a combination of thoughts, body sensations, and emotions. Those thoughts, body sensations, and emotions that lead to a big anger reaction are likely remnants of the past. The overwhelming past experiences that didn't move through your brain are likely the source of a big anger reaction. If you believe that strong anger reactions are a result of past, unprocessed experiences, that is a very large first step. If you just got this message from this book, it can be very healing. If you recognize that anger stems from past experiences, you can observe your reaction, which allows you a little space to have a different reaction. If you combine that observation with a reminder that what you are reacting to is not happening now but from the past, that is even more helpful. The awareness that you are actually reexperiencing a fragment of the past can help lessen the intensity of anger reactions.

Some resources for increasing mindful awareness:

- Noticing the present moment is a powerful, simple way to increase awareness. Here are some easy ways to practice being aware of this moment:
    - Watching a bird build a nest or something else out in nature.
    - Noticing if the temperature of the air changes from going in through your nose to coming out through your nose.
    - Smelling something pleasant like peppermint.
    - Spending time with a pet.
    - Taking a shower and noticing the feeling of the water.
- Taking five minutes a day to be aware of your breath going in and out of your nostrils can be a way to calm your mind.
- Spending time in nature can be a helpful way to increase mindful awareness. It is especially helpful if you are able to be silent as you are in nature. The quiet beauty of nature makes it easier to practice mindful awareness. This may include being in the woods, sitting by the ocean, or even finding a place to view the stars at night.

- Vipassana meditation offers ten-day meditation courses. They are free and offered all over the world. You can get information on the website www.dhamma.org.
- Yoga is an ancient spiritual meditation practice. Mostly viewed as a form of exercise in the Western world, true yoga is about freedom from old patterns of the mind and body.
- There are many different types of meditation that are very helpful in decreasing stress and increasing awareness.

Compassionate Assumption Toward Others

"When I am irritated by the behaviors or actions of other people, I can take a moment to recognize it is likely an activation of their past unhealed wounds. I can have compassion for the pain that fuels their reactions."

Practicing compassion may be the most helpful thing you can do to heal problematic anger. Instead of judging others as "crazy" when you do not understand their reaction, assuming that the reaction was once helpful for them and is here because of their unhealed past experiences can be helpful.

Having a compassionate assumption is about recognizing that people are doing the best they can with what they have to work with. Being a human is not an easy thing. We have all developed strategies for helping us feel protected and connected. These strategies once served us to maximize connection and protection. They now often create unhelpful patterns and behaviors that keep us from authentic connection and recognizing we are safe now.

Practicing a compassionate assumption toward others is not about condoning their behavior. It is more about helping you let go of things you cannot change and creating a peaceful internal world. Utilizing a compassionate assumption can minimize your stress response and reduce the release of stress hormones, which are known to create many unhealthy side effects. In fact, a feeling of compassion helps you to feel more relaxed and peaceful.

Compassionate Assumption Toward Yourself

"When I experience a behavior or reaction that I later regret, I have an opportunity to change the pattern by offering myself a compassionate assumption."

For most people, it is easier to offer others a compassionate response than it is to be compassionate toward themselves.

What if your negative reaction to yourself is actually fueling the pattern you want to stop? Self-compassion can help you to soften your reaction toward the hurt parts of you. Remember, compassion is not about avoiding responsibility or condoning hurtful behavior; it's about a deep desire to live a more peaceful, kind life, and being willing to apply that peace and kindness to yourself.

Healthy Boundaries

"I recognize my right to set clear boundaries."

Being able to set clear boundaries in a timely manner is key to living a peaceful life. Healthy boundaries are about recognizing your rights and the rights of others. There are many ways that healthy boundaries are helpful.

Saying no clearly without explaining. Feeling the need to explain your no to someone can open the door to them trying to problem solve for you. For example, a family member asks you to watch their pet while they are on vacation and you don't want to. Instead of just saying no, you might say something like, "I'm sorry but I can't. I have to work all day." Then the family member might say, "Oh, that's fine. He is used to being home alone all day, he won't mind." Now what? It is much easier to just be clear from the beginning and clearly state something like this: "No, I can't help you. I hope you find someone."

Healthy boundaries are also about not feeling like you have to problem solve for others. Doing that may sound like this: "No, I can't. Have you thought of boarding him at the kennel?" Problem solving for other people is a common way boundaries are violated. Giving unsolicited advice or believing you need to rationalize your choices regarding any unwanted advice from others are examples of unhealthy boundaries. Recognizing your right to say no and not explaining why is an important skill that is vital for a peaceful life.

Unspoken agreements. It can be very helpful for you to look at your relationships and their unspoken agreements. Is there a relationship that you would like to feel better about? Are you taking responsibility for things in a relationship that don't feel like they should be yours?

Unhealthy boundaries can creep up on you over time. Maybe what you agreed to years ago doesn't feel right to you anymore. However, even if you don't explicitly agree to your current relationship patterns, you are still maintaining them by silently continuing to play your part.

It can be helpful to journal about your current agreements. After you have written down the current patterns, take some time to decide and write about what you would like for a new agreement. If you are feeling resentful about your current relationship patterns and agreements, the relationship is suffering. The other party may breathe a sigh of relief when you adopt new, healthier boundaries. It may also be that the other person doesn't like the new agreement, but as long as you are deciding what is right for you and not demanding that the other person change, it is setting a healthy boundary.

Finding an EMDR Professional

If this book has motivated you to find an EMDR professional, there are some important things to ask and look for.

Ask the professional what percentage of the time they use EMDR in their practice. There are many people trained in EMDR, but they are not all equal. Some professionals get the initial EMDR training and advertise that they are trained, but rarely use it. If you want the best results, find a clinician who states they use EMDR with all or most of their clients.

Ask if they are EMDRIA Certified. EMDR International Association (EMDRIA) is the professional organization for EMDR clinicians. After taking the initial six-day training, a clinician has the option to become EMDRIA certified. A clinician who has completed certification has taken the next step toward being an EMDR expert.

If you resonate with the SAFE approach to EMDR in this book, you may want to visit http://www.safeemdr.com.

References

Dolezal, L., and M. Gibson. 2022. "Beyond a Trauma-Informed Approach and Towards Shame-Sensitive Practice." *Humanities and Social Sciences Communications* 9 (214).

Jarero, I., and L. Artigas. 2009. "EMDR Integrative Group Treatment Protocol." *Journal of EMDR Practice and Research* 3 (4): 287–288.

Karpman, S. 1968. "Fairy Tales and Script Drama Analysis." *Transactional Analysis Bulletin* 7 (26): 39–43.

Kearney, B. E., and R. A. Lanius. 2022. "The Brain-Body Disconnect: A Somatic Sensory Basis for Trauma-Related Disorders." *Frontiers in Neuroscience* 16: 1015749.

Kearney, B. E., B. A. Terpou, M. Densmore, S. B. Shaw, J. Théberge, R. Jetly, M. C. McKinnon, and R. A. Lanius. 2023. "How the Body Remembers: Examining the Default Mode and Sensorimotor Networks During Moral Injury Autobiographical Memory Retrieval in PTSD." *NeuroImage: Clinical* 38: 103426.

McCraty, R. 2017. "New Frontiers in Heart Rate Variability and Social Coherence Research: Techniques, Technologies, and Implications for Improving Group Dynamics and Outcomes." *Frontiers in Public Health* 5: 267.

Shapiro, F. 2017. *Eye Movement Desensitization and Reprocessing (EMDR) Therapy: Basic Principles, Protocols, and Procedures* (3rd ed.). New York: Guilford Press.

Shapiro, F. 2013. *Getting Past Your Past: Take Control of Your Life with Self-Help Techniques from EMDR Therapy*. New York: Rodale Books.

Deborah S. Kennard, LLP, is a leading expert on eye movement desensitization and reprocessing (EMDR) therapy. She is CEO and founder of the Personal Transformation Institute (PTI), one of the largest EMDR training institutes offering live and online learning to clinicians throughout the world. Kennard developed somatic and attachment-focused EMDR (SAFE), which expands on Shapiro's original EMDR model. She holds a master's degree in clinical psychology from Eastern Michigan University. Kennard connects with her community by offering live monthly webinars.

MORE BOOKS from NEW HARBINGER PUBLICATIONS

THE COGNITIVE BEHAVIORAL WORKBOOK FOR ANGER

A Step-by-Step Program for Success

978-1684034321 / US $24.95

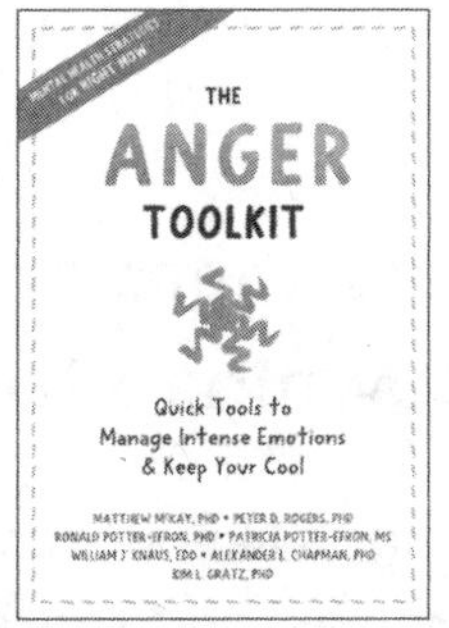

THE ANGER TOOLKIT

Quick Tools to Manage Intense Emotions and Keep Your Cool

978-1648481338 / US $16.95

THE POLYVAGAL SOLUTION

Vagus Nerve-Calming Practices to Soothe Stress, Ease Emotional Overwhelm, and Build Resilience

978-1648484124 / US $19.95

THE EMDR WORKBOOK FOR TRAUMA AND PTSD

Skills to Manage Triggers, Move Beyond Traumatic Memories, and Take Back Your Life

978-1684039586 / US $24.95

EMDR FOR ANXIETY

Powerful Self-Guided Tools for Overcoming Panic, Fear, Stress, and Worry

978-1648484896 / US $19.95

THE DIALECTICAL BEHAVIOR THERAPY SKILLS WORKBOOK FOR ANGER

Using DBT Mindfulness and Emotion Regulation Skills to Manage Anger

978-1626250215 / US $25.95

new**harbinger**publications

1-800-748-6273 / newharbinger.com

(VISA, MC, AMEX / prices subject to change without notice)

Follow Us

Don't miss out on new books from New Harbinger.
Subscribe to our email list at **newharbinger.com/subscribe**